DATE			

DISCARD

Arab Foreign Aid

Arab
Foreign Aid_____

Andre Simmons

Rutherford • Madison • Teaneck
Fairleigh Dickinson University Press
London and Toronto: Associated University Presses

Associated University Presses, Inc.
4 Cornwall Drive
East Brunswick, New Jersey 08816

Associated University Presses Ltd.
69 Fleet Street
London EC4Y 1EU, England

Associated University Presses
Toronto, Ontario, Canada M5E 1A7

Library of Congress Cataloging in Publication Data

Simmons, Andre.
   Arab foreign aid.

   Bibliography: p.
   Includes index.
   1. Economic assistance, Arab. I. Title.
HC498.S55   338.91′17′4927   80-65281
ISBN 0-8386-3019-7

Printed in the United States of America

Contents

Preface
Acknowledgments
Introduction   11

Part 1: National Programs

1. Kuwait   35
2. Saudia Arabia   58
3. United Arab Emirates   66
4. Iraq, Libya, and Qatar   78

Part 2: Multinational Programs

5. Arab Bank for Economic Development in Africa
   (ABEDA)   91
6. Arab Fund for Economic and Social Development
   (AFESD)   109
7. Islamic Development Bank (I.D.B.)   122
8. The OPEC Special Fund   131
9. Special Arab Fund for Africa (SAAFA)   143
10. OAPEC Special Account for the Arab Petroleum-
    Importing Countries (SAAPIC)   146
Conclusions   150
Appendix—Tables   173
Bibliography   185
Index   193

Preface

The unexpected increase in the prices of petroleum by the Organization of the Petroleum Exporting Countries (OPEC) in October and December of 1973 introduced a totally new element into the international economic relations. The 400-percent increase in the prices of oil exerted a sudden and significant impact upon all countries of the world. It affected also the developing nations of Africa and Asia. Frequently, it is believed that the impact upon the developing nations has been much greater than the impact on the countries of Europe and North America. According to a recent study presented in the *Middle East Yearbook 1977*, "The impact of the quadrupling of oil prices has been far more severe on the balance of payments and foreign resources of the non-oil-producing developing countries than on Europe or Japan."*

At the same time as the importers of oil were confronted with very serious difficulties on their balances of international trade, the oil-exporting countries, being unable to spend a major part of their oil revenues, began to accumulate large surpluses of the so-called petro-dollars. Thus a new situation was created in the arena of international economic and financial relations. A massive transfer of financial resources to a small group of nations from the rest of the world has upset the financial stability of the world

The Middle East Yearbook (Centre for Middle Eastern and Islamic Studies, University of Durham, England), 1977, p. 60.

economy and has exerted its impact on all members of the world community. To prevent any further deterioration of the situation, and in order to restore some of the stability to the international markets, several measures had to be undertaken. Different countries reacted in different ways, and a large number of policies were introduced, aiming essentially at a restoration of equilibrium to the international markets confronted by a new set of conditions, following the new prices of oil. One of the new policies that were launched following the events of 1973 was the program of foreign economic aid provided by the Arab exporters of oil to the developing nations of Africa and Asia. This study presents an examination of various aspects of this program, and several specific policies of the Arab aid program are analyzed. In the first part of this study a review is presented of the efforts made by the governments of various Arab states to initiate *national* programs of foreign assistance. The second part of this study focuses its attention on the *multilateral* and *multinational* efforts. It discusses the formation and the operation of several inter-Arab funds that attempted to channel the flow of petro-dollars contributed jointly by the Arab countries to the emerging nations in Africa and Asia.

Finally, a review of the effectiveness of the Arab foreign aid and the directions of its future trends is presented. An attempt is made to ascertain whether the Arab foreign assistance represents a short-term, transient phenomenon, resulting from a coincidental aggregation of special circumstances, or whether it will continue for the foreseeable future and make its durable impact on the path of future economic growth of the developing nations on the continents of Africa and Asia.

Introduction

The sudden fourfold increase in the prices of oil decided by the OPEC in the fall of 1973 had a very profound effect on all countries of the world. The increase in the price from approximately \$3 a barrel to almost \$12 in October and December 1973, introduced a new element into the international economic relations and has upset the monetary stability of the world. New measures and new policies had to be initiated in order to deal with a new situation confronting the world economy. One of the new policies introduced at that time by the Arab countries exporting oil was the foreign assistance program offering aid to the developing countries of Africa and Asia.

It was believed that a large-scale injection of Arab money into the economies of those countries will help them partially to overcome the difficulties created by the new prices of oil, and at the same time will assist them in the implementation of their development plans and projects.

A question has been frequently asked concerning the motives that prompted the Arab states to offer economic assistance to the developing nations. Obviously, any discussion of motives behind any policy of any country in the area of international economic relations, as much as in the area of international politics, is highly speculative, and any conclusions reached are rather tentative and should be approached with a certain degree of caution. Even if it is impossible to ascertain precisely the motivation behind the Arab foreign aid, nevertheless a number of definite ele-

11

ments that contributed to the decision to launch the foreign aid program could be detected.

Undoubtedly, many of those elements were based essentially on economic grounds. The developing countries needed assistance in general; they needed it even more when confronted with the balance of payments difficulties following the increase in their import expenditures on oil. Their deficits were growing very rapidly while at the same time the surpluses of the OPEC members were increasing equally rapidly also. There were numerous studies made in the past few years that very clearly demonstrate the relation between the growing deficits of the African and Asian nations, and the growing surpluses of the OPEC group.[1]

A meeting of the International Bank (I.B.R.D.) and the International Monetary Fund (I.M.F.), held in Manila in October 1976, analyzed the economic consequences of the increasing prices of oil upon the world economy and the international liquidity. One of the studies presented at that meeting concluded that "the most troubling part of the picture is the impact on the less developed nations, which, since the 400 percent OPEC price increases of three years ago, have run up a total of about $100 billion in balance-of-payments deficits."[2] This top-heavy debt of the poor nations was a source of increasing concern to the I.M.F. officials. Many expressed their apprehensions that "another oil price rise would increase the likelihood that some of those debts will have to be stretched out, or there will be defaults."[3]

A recent study presented by the I.M.F. summarized the international financial situation that developed since 1973 in the table below.[4] The figures cover a period of three years: 1974–76.

Similar conclusions were also reached by a study conducted by the United Nations Conference on Trade and Development (UNCTAD). This study was primarily concerned with a group of countries that are at the bottom of

COMBINED SURPLUSES   1974–76

OPEC	$142 billion
USA, Japan, Germany	26 billion
Benelux, Switzerland	12 billion
Total	$180 billion

COMBINED DEFICITS

France, U.K., Canada, Italy	$ 50 billion
Other industrial countries	50 billion
Developing nations	80 billion
Total	$180 billion

the scale in terms of income per capita, and are officially referred to as the MSA countries (the Most Seriously Affected). According to that study, the combined total deficit of forty-two MSA countries increased from $2.8 billion in 1973 to $12 billion in 1974.[5] Another study also conducted by UNCTAD analyzed the impact of the new oil prices on the developing nations in general and concluded that the total deficits of 113 non-oil-producing developing countries increased from $12.2 billion in 1973 to $33.5 billion in 1974, and to $45 billion in 1975.[6] The UNCTAD study was also seriously concerned about the rapidly increased debt-service charges that are facing the developing nations. According to UNCTAD estimate, the debt-service payments of the developing countries in Africa in 1974 represented fifty percent of their total combined current account deficit.[7]

Another study conducted by the International Bank expressed its opinion that "the prospects for the LDC's (Less Developed Countries) are at their lowest ebb in two decades. The LDC's will have to choose between defaulting on their debt payments and squeezing their economies to cut import demand. A cut in the consumption would be difficult, so it is bound to be investments that suffer most. This in turn will slow down growth."[8]

The conclusion reached by the I.M.F., UNCTAD, and I.B.R.D. studies were exceedingly disturbing and created a great deal of concern among the politicians and economists. Those conclusions offered very limited prospects for economic growth in the developing countries in the immediate future. Equally disturbing have been some of the reports based on studies undertaken by private independent organizations. In October 1976, the *Newsweek* magazine published its semiannual "World Economic Forecast."[9] According to this forecast, in 1975 the African export prices declined by 9 percent while the volume of African exports declined by 4 percent. At the same time, the prices of African imports increased by 45 percent in 1974 and by 12 percent in 1975. The African nations were therefore squeezed between the decreasing export earnings and rapidly increasing payments for imports. The outcome of this squeeze was obvious: a mounting volume of foreign debts. The *Newsweek* study concluded that "prospects are for stagnant per capita income performance in Africa for the rest of the 1970's."[10]

It can be safely assumed that the rapidly deteriorating economic position of the developing nations, and their equally rapidly disappearing chances for any significant economic progress in the 1970s, played an important role in the decision of the Arab nations to initiate the foreign aid program.

In addition to those purely economic considerations, there were many political elements involved in the decision to offer assistance to the developing nations. It is generally believed that, following the October 1973 war, the Arab nations tried to mobilize the world opinion behind their policy of confrontation with Israel. They attempted to mobilize it within the United Nations and also on any other conceivable political forum. It was expected that the flow of economic aid will help to establish not only closer economic contacts, but also closer political relations between the donors and the recipients of the aid. The OPEC members believed, and probably quite correctly, that the increasing economic power stemming from the surpluses of the petro-dollars will help them to assert an increasing political influence on the stage of international diplomacy. The links established by the flow of economic assistance will be transformed into solid political links in international relations. Looking back at the events of the past few years, it could be concluded that, in general, the Arab nations have succeeded in forging stronger links with the African and Asian nations, and furthermore, they have also succeeded in exercising much stronger influence in the international politics.

More probably, an additional, third element has been present in the formulation of the Arab foreign aid policy. This element could be best defined as the growing solidarity between the nations of the so-called Third World. This policy of solidarity has been manifested on numerous occasions by a multitude of policies pursued by various agencies of the United Nations.[11] Since the early 1960s, the United Nations Organization has consistently followed a policy of strengthening the cooperation and collaboration between the emerging nations of the Third World. This policy found its expression in constant efforts undertaken by the Economic Commission for Africa, Economic Commission for Asia, United Nations Industrial Development Organization, Food and Agriculture Organization, UNCTAD, GATT, and many others. Most recently this policy has been manifested in huge international conferences organized by the UNCTAD in Mexico City in September 1976, and in Nairobi (Kenya) in 1977. The general goal of those meetings was to discuss specific measures that the developing nations could jointly undertake in order to speed up the rate of their economic progress.[12] The initiative for calling the conference in Mexico City originated in a meeting of ministers of the developing nations, frequently referred to as the Group of 77. The resolution presented at that meeting was subsequently endorsed by the UNCTAD, and a decision was taken to call an international conference that would explore all possible means and measures that would tend to increase economic cooperations between the developing countries. Finally, the conference met for about two weeks in September 1976, and representatives of eighty-six countries were attending.[13] A substantial volume of various studies was presented. One of the main points stressed by those studies was the increased emphasis on cooperation among the developing countries rather than their reliance on aid from the industrialized nations. It was argued that frequently the self-aid of the developing nations may be more effective in stimulating growth than the economic assistance provided from outside the Third world.

Thus the policy of the Arab nations to offer aid to the developing nations in Africa and Asia was not only within the framework of the long-established policies of the United Nations, but it found also its immediate and wholehearted approval of all United Nations agencies. This approval was indicated not only in speeches on the floors of various U.N. assemblies, but it was also demonstrated in tangible forms by providing all kinds of technical and professional assistance that would make that aid more efficient and more effective.

Finally, it ought to be kept in mind that the policy of foreign aid from the Arab to the African nations was not only within the framework of the United Nations' policy on economic cooperation among the developing nations. More specifically, it was also within the framework of the policy aiming at Afro-Arab unity.

Since the early 1960s, when most of the African nations

gained their independence, the Organization of African Unity, as a representative of the newly independent African continent, has consistently advocated a policy of forging the closest possible links with the Arab League, and with the Arab nations in general. The newly independent nations in sub-Saharan Africa have continuously tried to form a solid link with the Arab countries in North Africa, most of which have enjoyed independence already prior to the 1960s. As those North African Arab countries were part of the larger Arab world, most of the African leaders believed that serious attempts should be made to forge an Afro-Arab community based on permanent, solid, and effective foundations. A climactic point of the growth of Afro-Arab unity was reached at the Afro-Arab Summit Meeting in Cairo, March 1977.[14] At that meeting, the leaders of over sixty independent African and Arab nations pledged to strengthen their bonds by developing a multitude of specific projects and programs, based on joint effort. In addition, Saudi Arabia, Kuwait, and the United Arab Emirates, as representatives of the Arab world, have offered $1.5 billion in economic aid to the sub-Saharan African nations. It should be also mentioned that the Afro-Arab unity is based not only on political proclamations and on speeches made at international gatherings. It is based on solid facts. A recent study, while discussing the basis for the Afro-Arab cooperation, stressed the fact that "more than 60 percent of all Arab people live in Africa and about 50 percent of Africa's population is Arab."[15] Thus, both the Arab and the African countries looked upon the Arab foreign aid as a symbol of Afro-Arab unity and also as a cornerstone that would enable them to join their efforts and to build collectively an effective base for their future economic, social, and political progress.

As mentioned earlier, the relationship between the new prices for oil and the economic situation in the developing countries has been the subject of many studies in recent years. One of the most recent and also most analytical discussions of the impact of the fourfold increase in the prices of oil on the newly independent nations of Africa and Asia was presented by Dr. Yoon Park.[16] In his view there exists a basic and fundamental difference between the impact of higher prices of oil upon the industrialized nations and upon the LDCs (Less Developed Countries). This major difference concerns the problem of recycling and of transfer. As the surplus of the petro-dollars has to be placed somewhere, either in physical assets or in financial assets, the recycling process takes place more or less automatically. However, as those real or financial assets are located almost exclusively in the industrial or financial centers of Europe, Japan, or the United States, the recycling process takes place only in those countries simply because they have something to recycle, either in the form of exports or real assets located at home (real estate, factories, etc.) or financial assets (stocks, bonds, banks, etc.). The recycling, however, does not take place with the LDCs simply because they have nothing, or very little, to recycle with the OPEC nations. As there has been in the past, and most probably will continue to be, very little direct contact between the OPEC and the LDCs, an alternative approach, containing an intermediary step or channel, has to be used. Such an intermediary could be either in the form of the I.M.F. Healey Plan, or the I.M.F. Whiteveen Plan, or it could be also in the form of Arab aid (grants and loans) to a developing nation.[17] The financial aid provided by the Arab countries could help to pay for the capital goods and the technical assistance provided by the U.S.A. or a European nation. Thus a trilateral system could be developed, based on Arab money, African natural resources, and European technology. Such a system would serve then as a mechanism used to "recycle" the petro-dollars to the less developed countries. Dr. Park is convinced that the "burden of the OPEC trade surplus falls more heavily on non-oil developing countries than on the industrial countries."[18] This heavier impact is caused by the fact that the developing countries cannot reduce their demand for imports of oil, while at the same time the cost of imported fertilizers and other petrochemicals used in agriculture have gone up. To aggravate the situation further, the terms of trade are moving against the tropical countries. In the final analysis, Dr. Park feels very strongly that the prospects for any significant improvement in the economic situation of tropical Africa and South Asia during this century are very bad indeed. The only thing that may somewhat alleviate the situation temporarily, but not correct it completely, is foreign aid. "In the absence of such capital flows, non-oil developing countries may be forced to abandon any hope of achieving even a modicum of economic growth in the coming decade," Dr. Park believes.[19] On the basis of his studies, he concluded that "perhaps the most serious economic effect of the sharp increase in oil prices has been felt by those countries that are least able to afford such an increase, that is the non-oil developing. . . . It is this group of countries that is likely to spark an economic disaster on international scale, if there is to be one."[20] The conclusions and the apprehensions expressed by Dr. Park have been also confirmed by another study prepared by Mr. Michael Field, and published under somewhat sensational title "A Hundred Million Dollars a Day."[21] Mr. Field is totally convinced that foreign aid is the only practical way of recycling the petro-dollars back to the developing nations.

Most of the discussions and the majority of statistical data concerning the flows of the petro-dollars, the accumulation of surpluses, and the flows of foreign aid refer to all OPEC members rather than to the Arab exporters only. At the moment, the membership in the OPEC consists of seven

Arab countries (Saudi Arabia, Iraq, Kuwait, Qatar, Libya, the U.A.E., and Algeria) and six non-Arab countries (Venezuela, Iran, Indonesia, Nigeria, Ecuador, and Gabon). From the point of view of the issues discussed in this study, however, the difference between the OPEC members and the Arab members of that organization has a rather limited practical significance. While it is true that the export earnings of the Arab members represent only a part of the total earnings of all OPEC members, nevertheless it is equally true that the majority of the OPEC members have never succeeded in accumulating any significant surpluses. Indonesia and Nigeria have large populations and equally large financial needs for their own development programs. The total earnings of countries such as Gabon, Ecuador, and Venezuela have been relatively modest and could be very easily spent either at home or on small-scale investments abroad. Their temporary surpluses were very minor. It is, therefore, only the Arab countries and Iran, among the OPEC members, that have been experiencing the accumulation of the surpluses of petro-dollars following the events of 1973. More recently, however, even the surpluses of Iran started to disappear. Due to a large population base and to almost unlimited needs of its own development plans, combined with huge military expenditures, Iran ceased to be a creditor nation already in 1977. Furthermore, even prior to that year, Iran had never attempted to launch a definite program of foreign assistance. Thus, it is only the Arab members of OPEC, with their massive oil revenues combined with a very limited population base, that had any significant volumes of surpluses of petro-dollars that could be partially channeled into various assistance programs. From the practical point of view, therefore, the "OPEC foreign assistance" and the "Arab foreign assistance" are essentially identical. According to the data presented in a recent United Nations study, Arab donors accounted for

100 percent of the total OPEC aid in 1973, for 75 percent in 1974, and for 85 percent in 1975 and 1976.[22] The remaining percentages represent some temporary, occasional grants of foreign assistance by Iran and Venezuela. As mentioned above, however, starting in 1977, Iran ceased to accumulate any surpluses, and thus the limited flow of assistance stopped completely. Venezuela still continues to provide a limited flow of what is officially classified as "foreign assistance." A closer examination would reveal, however, that most of those grants have the character of purely commercial transactions or commerical investments, and are limited to the neighboring Latin American countries only.[23]

In recent years there have been numerous studies, reports, and investigations presented by various international institutions, such as the I.M.F., I.B.R.D., OECD, and BIS, or by the leading American and European banking houses, such as the First National City Bank of New York, the Irving Trust Company, and the Morgan Guaranty Trust Company of New York, trying to determine the volumes of the surpluses of the petro-dollars and also the magnitude of the Arab foreign aid. In addition, of course, the leading economic and financial journals and magazines also tried to present their estimates and their analysis of the Arab foreign assistance programs. Even a brief examination of those studies, reports, and articles would immediately reveal that there exists a rather wide divergence between those estimates.

There are several reasons that most probably could account for a major part of this divergence. First of all, there is no unanimous agreement as to what constitutes foreign aid. Is a loan offered for fifteen years at 6 percent interest by an institution in one country to another country a regular commercial transaction or is it part of foreign aid? The definitions recently adopted by various agencies of the

United Nations, and their classification of concessionary and nonconcessionary loans, do not really help very much to clarify the concepts. An argument could be probably presented that a nonconcessionary assistance is not assistance at all, but simply a commercial transaction.

The second reason accounting for the differences in various estimates is more complicated. Are the estimates based on actual disbursements of money, or are they based on formal commitments expressed by signing an official loan agreement, or are they based on various press releases supplied by official or semiofficial agenices, or, finally, are they calculated on the basis of statements made in public announcements by various political leaders? It appears that some estimates have been based on the actual disbursements of cash, while others were made on the basis of formal commitments, officially announced.

Probably one example will illustrate the nature of this problem. At the first Afro-Arab Summit Meeting in Cairo, March 7–9, 1977, in response to the Zambian request for $2 billion in aid in order to compensate for the increased price of oil, the government of Saudi Arabia announced an offer of one billion dollars in aid to Africa.[24] Subsequently, this offer was supplemented by an additional one-half billion dollars of aid by Kuwait, Abu Dhabi, and Qatar.[25] Thus an official announcement was made at a formal gathering of leaders of over sixty African and Arab states. Needless to add that this announcement made big headlines all over the world. However, it was never stated when this aid will be forthcoming, to whom it will be offered, under what conditions, for what purpose, and who will control it. Will it be in the form of investment capital for specific projects, or will it be a general balance-of-payments support program? Will this $1.5 billion be in addition to the aid currently offered or are the present commitments already included in this offer? The lack of specific answers and the uncertainties about the specific aspects of the announced aid may account for serious differences in the estimates. Should the offer of $1.5 billion be counted as part of Arab aid to Africa in 1977?[26]

Another source of divergence between various estimates concerns the so-called Whiteveen Facility, an I.M.F. credit facility based on joint contributions from the OPEC members (45 percent) and the importers of oil (55 percent).[27] The essential idea behind this plan was to offer credit facility to countries that may be experiencing balance of payments' difficulties caused by large payments for the imports of oil. Saudi Arabia made the largest single contribution to that fund ($2.4 billion), and other OPEC members also contributed substantial amounts. As the loans from the Whiteveen Facility will be offered to all countries, developed as well as undeveloped, there appears to be a difference of opinion as to whether or not the OPEC contribution should be considered as part of foreign aid. Some publications, when discussing the Arab foreign aid, clearly identify the contributions made to the Whiteveen Facility as a separate item, some include it as part of the regular aid, while others ignore it completely, without even mentioning it.

Finally, it is generally believed that the official announcements about the commitments or disbursements of aid cover only one part of the total aid. It is frequently assumed that part of the Arab aid is never fully disclosed in a detailed way; it can only be estimated in an indirect fashion. Considering the fact that, in addition to economic motives, there are also political and military considerations behind the Arab foreign aid, such a situation should be easily understood. For example, a recent study of the contemporary economic situation in Saudi Arabia discussed the question of the Arab aid and concluded that "the exact distribution . . . is a closely held secret."[28] Although it is known that most of the aid goes to the confrontation states, "the amounts have never been published and the flow has never been regular."[29]

Although the flow of the Arab foreign aid started on a massive scale only in 1974, already prior to that year some Arab countries were allocating a substantial part of their oil revenues to the assistance offered to the developing countries. Historically, Kuwait was the first among the Arab countries to launch a program of foreign assistance. In 1961 it formed the Kuwait Fund for Arab Economic Development, and during the 1960s was regularly transferring every year about 6 to 7 percent of its G.N.P. to the fund.[30] Throughout the 1960s, the Kuwait Fund was the only example of this kind of financial assistance provided to the less fortunate Arab neighbors. In 1971, a second fund was created, by the government of Abu Dhabi, under the name of Abu Dhabi Fund for Arab Economic Development. The following year, a multinational institution, under the name of Arab Fund for Social and Economic Development, started its activities.

The events of 1973 marked a turning point in the history of economic relations between the Arab oil-exporting countries and the developing nations on the continents of Asia and Africa. Following a 400-percent increase in the price of oil, some of the Arab countries suddenly experienced a significant increase in their financial resources. Those resources enabled them to initiate massive plans of national economic development. In spite, however, of billions of dollars spent on the formation of their infrastructures and the development of the industrial sectors, most of the Arab oil exporters discovered that, due to limited capacity to absorb additional expenditures on the domestic scene, they started accumulating money faster than they could spend it. The term "surplus petro-dollars" was born. In turn, those surpluses provided the starting base for the large-scale economic aid to the developing nations in Africa and Asia.

A detailed examination of the sources and of the destinations as well as the magnitude of the Arab foreign aid is presented in the subsequent chapters of this study. Here, only a brief and general picture of the aid will be outlined. What are the main features of this aid? Is there anything that would differentiate Arab aid from, for example, American aid?

The flow of the Arab aid has been channeled through a large number of various outlets. A major part of this aid has been in the form of direct government-to-government grants and loans. Some of it has been offered through the newly formed institutions, such as, for example, the Islamic Development Bank, the Arab Bank for Economic Development in Africa, the Saudi Fund for development, and several other newly established funds. Part of this aid has been presented in the form of contributions to the well-established international agencies, frequently sponsored by the United Nations. In addition to the channels mentioned above, the Arab aid has also been granted in the form of co-financing of projects jointly with non-Arab sources, of establishing joint companies in foreign countries, and finally, in providing all sorts of banking and financing services such as guarantees, underwriting, etc.

Prior to 1973, the volume of the Arab aid was on a relatively modest scale.[31] Essentially, it was limited to grants and loans provided Kuwait, Libya, and Saudi Arabia to Jordan, Syria, and Egypt, and in 1972 the combined economic aid amounted to about $700 million. In 1974, the combined total Arab aid was estimated to equal $5.3 billion, according to UNCTAD calculations, or $4.7 billion, according to OECD figures. In addition to that, the Arab countries contributed $1.7 billion to the I.M.F. oil facility. In the following year, the aggregate Arab aid increased to about $6.6 billion, plus a contribution of $2.8 billion to the I.M.F.

As much as the absolute amounts of the Arab aid are very

impressive, even more impressive are the quantities of the aid expressed in relative terms, in relation, for example, to the G.N.P.

In 1975, Kuwait contributed 9.5 percent of its G.N.P. to the foreign aid, Qatar 8.1 percent, U.A.E. 7.4 percent, and Saudi Arabia 5.8 percent.[32] It may be interesting to compare those percentages with the percentages of the G.N.P. of the OECD countries that were channeled to foreign assistance. In spite of the fact that the United Nations proclaimed the decade of the 1970s as the "Decade of Development," and recommended that each country should aim at offering at least one percent of its G.N.P. in foreign aid, this target was achieved only occasionally by one or two countries. For most of the decade, the average for the majority of the OECD nations was around 0.7 percent. Thus in terms of percentage of the G.N.P. offered in foreign assistance, the aid provided by the Arab countries has been very likely ten times larger than the aid supplied by the developed nations. The gap is even wider when the aid is expressed in terms of per capita in the donor countries. It appears that the Arab aid has been between twenty-five and thirty times greater than the aid provided by the OECD group, when calculated in per capita terms.

Following the events of 1973, not only the absolute and the relative volumes of the Arab aid have increased, but also the number of contributors and the number of aid channels multiplied very rapidly. As mentioned above, prior to 1973 only Saudi Arabia, Kuwait, and Libya were able to offer any meaningful amounts of assistance. After 1973, the ranks of contributors were joined by almost all OPEC members, even if the contributions of some of them were rather nominal and only temporary. At the same time as the number of contributors was rising, so did the number of channels. Several new, national and multinational, institutions were created to provide regular and permanent arrangement for the flow of aid. A detailed discussion of those institutions is presented in the subsequent parts of this study. One of the interesting aspects of the Arab foreign aid is the direction of its flow. What countries are the major recipients of this aid? Although the press releases have a tendency to emphasize rather strongly the Arab aid to the *African countries,* and the subject of the Afro-Arab economic and political unity occupies a prominent place in various discussions and publications, nevertheless an examination of the data would reveal that actually a relatively small part of this aid is directed to Africa. According to a survey presented in the *Middle East Yearbook 1977,* and covering the period of five years between 1973 and 1977, 73 percent of the Arab aid went to other Arab countries; the Asian nations received 19 percent, while the African nations in the sub-Saharan Africa (that is, the non-Arab African nations) received only 8 percent.[33]

A more detailed analysis of the individual channels of the flow aid, presented in the subsequent parts of this study, will show that on the average about 90 percent of the aid directed to the Arab states was actually centered on three countries only, namely, Egypt, Syria, and Jordan. This means, in effect, that those three countries were the recipients of about two-thirds of the *total* Arab assistance. Among the Asian nations, by far the largest recipients of the aid were India, Pakistan, and Bangladesh.

As mentioned earlier, a precise calculation of the Arab foreign aid encounters several rather serious difficulties, and the margin of error in various estimates may be rather significant. Nevertheless, keeping those limitations in mind, an overall estimate of the Arab foreign assistance could be made, covering the period of five years starting with the year of 1974, when the large-scale aid program started, to the present year of 1978. Although at the time of this writing, the year 1978 had only started, nevertheless on the basis of numerous official statements and plans, a reasonably accurate projection could be made.

According to the available and reasonably reliable information, the total amount of aid provided by the Arab countries during the five-year period would most likely reach $30 billion. The bulk of this aid was provided by three countries (Saudi Arabia, Kuwait, and the U.A.E.), with a combined population of less than ten million people.

As a concluding observation, it may be interesting to underline that this amount of aid is very nearly identical with the total amount of aid provided by the U.S.A. during the same period. Considering, however, the fact that the population of the U.S.A. exceeds 200 million, the Arab aid is approximately twenty times larger in terms of per capita in the donor countries than the American aid.

Finally, there is one additional characteristic feature of the Arab foreign aid that is totally different from the features of foreign assistance provided by the United States or by the European countries. The origins of the American aid date back to World War II and to the Marshall Plan. The basic objective of the American aid was to supply the war-devastated European nations with capital goods that would enable them to rebuild their war-torn economies. The aid, therefore, took the form of a flow of goods. The dollars offered by the United States government were instantaneously recycled into goods produced by the American industry and agriculture. Even after the Marshall Plan ended in 1952, the U.S.A. aid continued to other parts of the world, and it still continues under the auspices of the Agency for International Development (AID). But, its basic character is always the same; what actually flows from the U.S.A. to the poor nations of Africa and Asia is the flow of goods. There is no problem of recycling. The foreign aid programs offered by England, France, and other OECD countries are essentially the same as the U.S.A. program.

The Arab aid, however, is *totally* different from the American or European aid. It represents only a flow of *financial* resources and not a flow of *real* resources. What moves is money, and not industrial goods, simply because the Arab donors, being themselves an underdeveloped nation, do not have industries and therefore cannot offer industrial goods. There is, therefore, the problem of recycling the dollars offered in aid by the Arab countries. The recycling takes place in the industrialized countries of the OECD group. Most of the dollars received by the African or Asian countries from OPEC will ultimately end in the German or French or American industries. Thus, in effect, those industries are enjoying part of the Arab foreign aid.

The difference between the Arab aid and the European or American aid could be summarized as follows: while the U.S.A. or the OECD aid in addition to benefiting the direct recipients of aid, also extended the benefits to the American or European industries supplying the capital goods, the Arab aid does not extend any extra benefits to the Arab industrial manufacturers. The extra benefits may go somewhere else.[34]

This conclusion could be restated by saying that the American or European aid had some elements of self-interest by promoting the exports of domestic products. The Arab aid is totally devoid of this kind of economic self-interest. There may be, of course, some political interest involved, but from the economic point of view the Arab aid is based on completely altruistic motives.

Notes

1. UNCTAD, *Recent Trends in International Trade and Development* (TD/186), May 1976, p. 2.

2. "Few Protest New Oil Price Rise," *International Herald Tribune*, 29 October 1976.

3. Ibid.
4. "Petro-Dollars Surpluses," *International Herald Tribune*, 24 February 1977.
5. UNCTAD (TD/186), p. 26.
6. UNCTAD, *International Financial Co-operation for Development*, (TD/188/Supp. 1), February 1976, p. 22.
7. UNCTAD (TD/188/Supp. 1), pp. 31–45.
8. "Oil and the Third World," *The Middle East*, February 1977, no. 28, p. 89.
9. "World Economic Forecast," *Newsweek*, 4 October 1976, p. 48.
10. Ibid, p. 54.
11. UNCTAD, *Economic Co-operation among Developing Nations* (TD/192 and Supp. 1 and Supp. 2), May 1976.
12. UNCTAD (TD/191/Supp. 1).
13. UNCTAD, *Report of the Conference on Economic Co-operation among Developing Countries* (77/COOP/CMEX/12), September 1976.
14. "Arabs, Africans Agree on Close Cooperation," *Arab News*, 10–11 March 1977.
15. "Arab-African Cooperation," *The Middle East*, December 1976, no. 26, p. 27.
16. Yoon S. Park, *Oil Money and the World Economy* (Boulder, Colo.: Westview Press, 1976).
17. Ibid., pp. 130–48.
18. Ibid., p. 153.
19. Ibid., p. 177.
20. Ibid., p. 178.
21. Michael Field, *A Hundred Million Dollars a Day* (London: Sidgwick and Jackson, 1975).
22. UNCTAD (TD/188/Supp. 1/Add. 1/Annex 1), p. 25.
23. UNCTAD (TD/192/Supp. 1).
24. "Afro-Arab Summit," *The Middle East*, April 1977, no. 30, p. 88.
25. "Africans at Summit Cheer as Saudis Pledge $1 Billion," *Arab News*, 8 March 1977; "Gulf States Add $453 m. in Aid for Black Africa," *Saudi Gazette*, 9 March 1977.
26. "First Right Step," *Arab News*, 9 March 1977.
27. "Strains on World Financial Systems Ease," *International Herald Tribune*, 27–28 August 1977.
28. "Foreign Aid Policy" (Focus on Saudi Arabia), *International Herald Tribune*, February 1978, p. 2.
29. Ibid.
30. OPEC Special Fund, *First Annual Report, 1976*.
31. Ibid.
32. Ibid.
33. *The Middle East Yearbook 1977*, p. 62.
34. OPEC Special Fund, p. 10.

Part 1
National Programs

1
Kuwait

Introduction

Following the increase in the prices of oil in 1973, Kuwait became one of the largest donors of foreign aid, not only among the Arab countries, but also when compared with the U.S.A. or the West European nations. This achievement is even more remarkable if one considers the fact that the population of Kuwait has not yet reached one million. The total volume of the flow of assistance to the developing countries increased from $550 million in 1973 to $1.711 billion in 1975 and to $1.875 in 1976.[1] In absolute terms, as far as the Arab countries are concerned, this magnitude of flow has been exceeded only by Saudi Arabia. In relative terms, that flow represented 9 percent of the G.N.P. in 1973 and it increased to 11.5 percent in 1975 and 1976. Those percentages were exceeded only by Qatar and U.A.E. in 1973 and 1975. In 1976, Kuwait's share of the G.N.P. allocated to foreign aid was the highest not only among the Arab states but, obviously, also the world.

In 1973, 1974, and 1975 the total volume of assistance was divided approximately evenly between the concessionary and the nonconcessionary types. In 1976, however, the share of the concessionary aid dropped to about 30 percent of the total aid, while the share of the nonconcessionary type increased to over 70 percent. During the three year period, 1973–75, between 80 and 90 percent of the concessionary aid was bilateral, while in 1976 the share of bilateral assistance decreased to about 60 percent. More than three-fourths of the bilateral assistance was directed to Egypt, Syria, and Jordan; the share of Egypt invariably exceeding the combined share of Syria and Jordan. In aggregate terms, the concessional form of aid as percentage of the G.N.P. increased from 5.7 percent in 1973 and 1974 to 6.5 percent in 1975, but dropped very significantly to 3.2 percent in 1976.

The volume of nonconcessional assistance increased from $205 million in 1973 to $628 million in 1974, and to $736 million in 1975. During the following year, 1976, it almost doubled to $1.348 billion. In all cases, almost all of the nonconcessional aid was bilateral, and Egypt was the principal recipient of this aid every year.[2]

An examination of the foreign assistance provided by Kuwait to the developing nations reveals very clearly that a major change in policy took place in 1976. While the total volume of aid registered only a very slight increase in terms of dollars, and no increase at all in terms of a percentage of the G.N.P., a major shift took place in the allocation of aid between the concessionary and the nonconcessionary forms. In 1975 and in all preceding years, the concessionary type of assistance has always exceeded the nonconcessionary type, while rather suddenly, in 1976, the nonconcessionary form of assistance became more than twice as large as the other type. In all cases, however, Egypt has remained the largest single recipient of aid from Kuwait. Such a change in the character of aid would most likely indicate that the Kuwait government has decided to change the emphasis of its aid from political and humanitarian motives to purely economic and commerical considerations.

If the general trend of the Kuwait aid observed in 1975 and 1976 could be projected into the future, it would appear that the volume of aid in terms of dollars as well as in terms of percentage of the G.N.P. may be leveling off to about $2 billion per year and 11.5 percent of the G.N.P.

Direct Governmental Aid

Most likely there is no other country in the world that could provide a more striking example of a successful management of the national economy that is based on one commodity only (i.e., oil) than Kuwait. With a population that is only now reaching one million inhabitants, Kuwait has attained one of the highest incomes per capita in the world. It reached the level of $11,000 in 1974 and in 1976 it increased to $16,300. The economy of the country is built on oil. The oil revenue in 1975 equaled $8.7 billion while in 1976 it declined slightly to $7.2 billion. Each year, the net surplus on the balance of trade amounted to approximately $4 billion.[3] Most of the surpluses were more or less equally divided between investments in real estate and in the stock exchanges of Europe and United States, and various forms of foreign assistance. The general guidelines of the policy of the Kuwait government was probably best expressed recently by a Kuwait minister. "The Kuwait Fund for Arab Economic Development and the Kuwait Government involvement in a large number of international and multinational financial organizations is largely done for political reasons . . . to be friendly with as many nations as possible."[4]

In addition to being one of the largest donors of foreign assistance in general, Kuwait has also been one of the largest contributors to various multinational agencies channeling the foreign aid. A major chance in the allocation of the Kuwait aid took place in 1976. Prior to that time, significantly less than 5 percent of total Kuwait aid was given to the multinational agencies; approximately 95 percent of it was of the bilateral character. In 1976, however, a basic change took place and the share of the multilateral assistance increased to 22 percent of the total aid. Even prior to that change, however, the role played by Kuwait in the financing of various multilateral Arab institutions has always been very substantial.

Kuwait has been the largest single subscriber to the Arab Fund for Economic and Social Development, the second largest subscriber to the Arab Fund for the Provision of Loans to African Countries, and a leading donor (21 percent) to the OPEC Special Fund. It also subscribed 8.7 percent of the capital of the Arab Bank for Economic Development of Africa and 13.3 percent of the capital of the Islamic Development Bank.

In addition to the financial flows that can be clearly identified as originating from the Kuwait government, it appears that there exists also an additional flow from several Kuwait business organizations that are largely owned and/or controlled by the government. For example, a large volume of foreign investments has originated from the Kuwait Investment Company (owned 50 percent by the government), from the Kuwait Foreign Trading Company (owned 80 percent by the government), and from the Afro-Arab Investment Company for Investment and Trade (owned 62 percent by the government). As the above mentioned companies are in effect either agencies of the Kuwait government or are directed by the government, it can be assumed that a large part of investments originating from those companies has actually originated from the government itself. There is, however, no way to ascertain precisely the magnitude of the flow of those investments in quantitative terms.[5]

In addition to the funds that can be clearly identified and classified as foreign assistance, Kuwait has also provided a substantial amount of money that, although officially not included in the foreign aid statistics, nevertheless is very similar to it, namely, the International Monetary Fund Oil Facility. During the three-year period, Kuwait offered over $900 million to that facility ($480 million in 1974, $243 million in 1975, and $186 million in 1976). Officially, the I.M.F. Oil Facility is not considered as an aid because the subscriptions to the facility remain as part of the subscriber's foreign exchange reserves. In attempting to discuss and to evaluate the magnitude of the foreign aid provided by Kuwait, there are several things that ought to be kept in mind. First, as Kuwait has been accumulating surpluses on its balance of trade for quite a number of years, the volume of Kuwait foreign investments and the size of the revenue originating from those investments are rather substantial. It has been estimated that in 1976 Kuwait received several hundred million dollars in revenues from its investments abroad made in the past.

The second thing that should be considered is the fact that it is rather difficult to obtain sufficient and reliable data concerning the finances, both domestic and foreign, of Kuwait. According to a survey conducted by the *Financial Times* (London), "Kuwait tends to be as tightlipped about its finances—both government and private—as other States are about their armed forces."[6] An additional complication arises from the very hazy dividing line between private and public finances and private and public foreign investments. Many foreign investment activities supposedly conducted by private banks and other financial institutions are in effect to a very large extent government transactions simply because the government is a part owner, frequently with a controlling vote, of most of those supposedly "private" banks. Furthermore, the dividing line between profit-making investment in a foreign country and financial assistance to that country is very vaguely defined. What one source may classify as "private foreign investment," another source may classify as "governmental foreign aid." Those factors explain to a large extent the discrepancies that frequently exist between the volumes of Kuwait foreign assistance, quoted by different sources. In general, the official Kuwait sources seem to have a tendency to classify "every conceivable kind of investment and both private and official loans" as foreign aid.[7] To reduce the risks involved, the Kuwait government has formed in August 1973 the Inter-Arab Investment Guarantee Corporation. It is believed that the formation of this corporation has a tendency of greatly increasing the flow of investments to Arab countries.

In 1976 Kuwait's activities in the Arab world included the formation of a joint investment company in Morocco with a capital of $50 million, a loan to Bahrain of $35 million, and another loan of $35 million to Algeria. In addition, Kuwait has also contributed $25 million to the Arab Monetary Fund, $20 million to the Arab Bank for Economic Development in Africa, and equally substantial amounts to the Islamic Development Bank and the Arab Fund for Economic and Social Development. Additional contributions were also made to the Special Fund of OPEC, to the Arab Petroleum Investment Company, and to the Fund for Arab Oil Importing Countries. Those three financial institutions were created after the fourfold increase in the price of oil in 1973–74, and were designed to alleviate the balance-of-payments difficulties of developing countries importing oil.

Kuwait started accumulating the surplus of petro-dollars at least a decade earlier than the other Middle East exporters of oil. Thus, the Kuwait government had the opportunity to have more experience and to develop more expertise in handling the flows of foreign assistance than the other Arab governments. Over a period of years, the government of Kuwait has also developed a set of certain attitudes and rules concerning foreign aid. Although those attitudes and ideas were never formally proclaimed as the official policy of the Kuwait government, nevertheless they were repeatedly stated on numerous occasions by Mr. Abdlatif Al-Hamad, the director general of the Kuwait Fund, and they could be considered as the policy of the Kuwait government.[8]

Probably the most important principle frequently stated has been the idea of closer economic cooperation between the Arab nations within the Middle East region. Since the mid-1960s the government has advocated the creation of formal and informal arrangements aiming at a more coordinated and more systematic network of economic relations, especially when the flows of capital and the problems of economic development were concerned. According to a study made by the Kuwait Fund, the "Middle East is the only region of the world that has not been able to follow the general trend towards the creation of a network of regional development institutions."[9]

To remedy this deficiency partly, the Kuwait government sponsored the establishment of the Inter-Arab Investment Guarantee Corporation and of the Arab Fund for Economic and Social Development. The first institution was aimed at facilitating the flow of private investments, while the second aimed at stimulating the flow of public investments. The government first presented the idea of the Arab Fund at the Summit Meeting in Khartoum in 1970, and when the Arab leaders approved it, the government contributed one-third of its capital.[10]

The second principle that emerged from the experience of handling the flow of Kuwait capital to foreign countries and especially to the underdeveloped areas was the belief that those flows should be looked upon not only from the humanitarian point of view but also from a purely commercial point of view. Namely, they should be considered also as investments that will provide Kuwait with a steady income in the future. There is no doubt that such a commercial approach has been adopted by Kuwait, and ultimately this objective proved to be very successfully accomplished. At the same time as Kuwait was stressing the financial and commercial objectives of its foreign assistance, it frequently expressed its conviction that money invested in the developing countries will not be able to accomplish very much unless it is closely connected with modern European or American technology.[11] Thus, Kuwait became gradually a firm believer in a trilateral cooperation among the natural resources of the developing nations, the financial resources provided by Kuwait, and modern Western technology.[12] The Kuwait leaders responsible for directing the flow of investments abroad expressed on numerous occasions their apprehensions that a significant amount of the investment capital will be wasted unless it is backed by solid feasibility studies, by marketing research, by modern machinery, and by proper management techniques. Kuwait obviously could not supply either the engineering expertise or the managerial capacity or the machinery. Therefore, the cooperation with the industrialized nations was believed to be essential.

In addition to expressing their faith in the cooperation with the industrialized nations, the Kuwait leaders also firmly believed in cooperation between the Arab nations donating the financial resources. Already in 1973, even prior to the time when the huge amounts of liquid capital began to accumulate in the Arab countries, Mr. Al-Hamad visualized the flow of Arab capital to African and Asian nations within a broad framework of cooperation, not only between the Arab donors, but also between the donors and various agencies of the United Nations.[13]

Although the Kuwait government was convinced that the flow of the Arab surplus capital to the developing nations is both unavoidable and essential, it adopted at the same time a very cautious, pragmatic, and frequently actually not a very enthusiastic attitude toward the ultimate effects of that flow. In a study prepared for the Kuwait government, Mr. Z. A. Nasr, an executive of the Kuwait Fund, stated that "awareness of the realities of the situation should caution us against excessive ambition."[14] In a paper presented at a conference sponsored by the OECD Development Center he expressed his view that

> be it as it may, we should above all beware of exuberant expectations. Trilateral cooperation, even if successfully institutionalized and active within the framework of some international New Deal, will not provide us with philosopher's stone capable of transforming poverty into affluence, backwardness into progress. . . . It is indeed a current self-deception in many LDC's to believe that extraordinary investment opportunities are there for the taking, and that it is only the reluctance of the foreigners or the timidity of petro-funds that prevents the blooming of the hidden capabilities and the take-off into prosperity. The grim spectacle of many structural bottlenecks . . . can easily recede into background . . . whenever . . . the wish is made master of the thought.[15]

The government of Kuwait seemed to have adopted a definite belief that the problems of development in Africa and in Asia will not be solved overnight and will not be solved by some "grand designs" or "grandiose schemes." Following this conviction, the government of Kuwait was never in favor of offering program lending but concentrated rather on project lending. It believed that project lending, although obviously less spectacular than program lending, will prove to be much more effective and more successful in the long run. In addition, it also believed that the number of profitable investment opportunities in the developing nations is rather limited, and any lending plan would require long preparation and long studies. Unfortunately, many African and Asian development programs lacked both long preparations and penetrating feasibility studies.

Finally, the Kuwait government believed that the most important first step toward assuring the success of the foreign assistance plans followed by the Arab countries with a surplus of petro-dollars was to adopt a coordinated approach and to try to attain the highest possible degree of collaboration in channeling their funds to the developing nations. The need for such a collaboration was strongly emphasized in a special study prepared by Dr. Ibrahim F. I. Shihata for the UNCTAD. He stated in May 1976 that "since January 1974 at least eighteen financial institutions with combined authorized capital of about $4 billion started operations as joint ventures among the Arab countries or between some of them (as the leading partners) and other developing countries."[16] Nonetheless, very little has been done so far to coordinate the activities of those eighteen institutions (and similar ones previously established). The attempts that have been made until now have been rather sporadic, not very enthusiastic, and therefore met with a very limited success.

Kuwait Fund for Arab Economic Development

The Kuwait Fund is one of the largest, oldest, and most successful institutions in the Arab world aiming at offering financial assistance to the developing countries. The history and the transformation of the fund are directly related to the political changes that took place in Kuwait. At the same time, the fund provides the first example in the Arab world of an institution channeling the flow of the surplus of petro-dollars toward investments outside of its own national boundaries.

The fund was established in December 1961, one year

after Kuwait gained its independence. At that time the basic objectives behind the formation of the fund were both political and economic. On the political level, the fund was used as a means of asserting the independence of Kuwait as a sovereign entity. On the economic level, the fund was aiming at promoting economic cooperation between the Arab states. There is no doubt that in 1961 the political elements were more decisive and more essential than the economic.[17] As soon as Kuwait declared her independence from the British protection, Iraq voiced her claims to the territory of Kuwait, and was preparing a military action against the newly independent state. Only the British military intervention prevented the occupation of Kuwait by the Iraqi army. By creating the fund, the government of Kuwait was attempting to draw the world's attention to its political independence, and at the same time to firmly establish itself as a member state of the Arab League. There is no doubt, as the subsequent experiences have amply demonstrated, that the Kuwait Fund has successfully accomplished those political objectives. After the unsuccessful invasion by Iraq, and after the British military intervention in 1961, the independence of Kuwait was never threatened again.

In addition to the political objectives, the formation of the fund also has its economic goals. The government of Kuwait, being fully aware that the relatively small population of its country would not be able to absorb the rapidly increasing revenues stemming from the exports of petroleum, attempted to create an institution that would enable it to channel the surplus funds to the neighboring Arab countries, and by doing so, to form closer economic relations with those countries.[18] The government also believed that by establishing closer economic and commercial contacts with its Arab neighbors, the spirit of the Arab solidarity and unity would be strengthened. The experience of the fund since 1961 very clearly demonstrates that during that period Kuwait proved to be one of the most generous donors of economic aid, both for development and also for humanitarian purposes. Between 1961 and 1973, the Kuwait foreign aid represented, on the average, about 15 to 20 percent of its annual budget, and about 7 percent of the G.N.P. During that period, Kuwait has earned about KD 2.8 billion (approximately $8 billion) from the export of oil, and has donated approximately one-fifth of it to foreign aid. During those years, a major part of the foreign aid was handled directly by the government, while the fund channeled a relatively minor part of it. Nonetheless, during those twelve years, the fund loaned KD 106 million to twelve Arab countries for over thirty different projects. Obviously, the scale of operations of the fund increased very significantly after 1973, following the quadrupling of the prices of oil.[19]

The present charter of the fund was originally adopted in April 1963, and was substantially amended in July 1974. According to the charter, the fund is an autonomous, independent body, governed by the board of directors, appointed by the government. Before 1974, the board was chaired by the finance minister, but after 1974 the chairmanship of the board of directors passed into the hands of the prime minister, who was also the crown prince of the State of Kuwait. Such an arrangement, undoubtedly, established a very close relation between the fund and the government.[20] The charter also provides that the board of directors should appoint a director-general of the fund, who is responsible for the day-to-day management and operation of the fund. Since 1962, Mr. Abdulatif Youssef Al-Hamad has occupied the position of the director-general of the fund, and there is ample evidence to suggest that the operations of the fund have been greatly influenced by the personality and conduct of Mr. Al-Hamad. An examination of the history of the fund would clearly reveal that his leadership and personality have left a definite imprint on the fund.[21] One of the characteristic features of the operations of the fund is the fact that the board of directors had invariably approved the recommendations and the plans submitted by Mr. Al-Hamad. So far, a fundamental conflict of views or a basic disagreement between the board of directors and the director-general has not developed.[22]

According to the original charter, the fund could lend only to the Arab states. The charter has been, however, modified and amended in 1974, and since that date the fund can provide financial assistance to any developing country. From the very beginning of its existence, the fund has adopted a set of rather definite rules concerning its lending policies. In approving loans, the fund has always been guided by the economic and financial considerations, and was disregarding all political pressures and motivations.

There were several types of financial aid provided by the fund in the 1960s. Most of the loans were granted for specific projects that were financially feasible and sound. The loans usually carried a rate of interest of 3 to 4 percent and were given for fifteen to twenty-five years. The amount of each loan never exceeded KD 10 million (about $35 million) and, also, never exceeded 50 percent of the total cost of the project. During the first decade of its operations, the fund granted thirty-eight loans to twelve Arab countries, totaling KD 106 million (about $350 million). Some of the projects for which loans were granted included power stations, phosphate mining, cement factories, highways, oil pipelines, irrigation projects, railways, sugar refining plants, grain silos, and repairs to the Suez Canal. The available evidence indicates that the fund has definitely adopted a policy of project lending, in preference to program lending.[23] Only very recently, the fund has slightly modified this policy by granting a limited number of loans to various national development banks that, most likely, will use the borrowed funds for the general development programs, rather than for specific projects only.

Kuwait Fund for Arab Economic Development

KD Millions

Fiscal Year	Loans	Technical Assistance Grants
1961–72	78.3	0.4
1972–73	9.0	0.3
1973–74	32.1	0.2
1974–75	41.6	1.2
1975 June-July	61.0	0.7
	222.0	2.8

(Note: Fund's fiscal year runs from June 1 to May 31.)

Source: United Nations Conference on Trade and Development, *Financial Cooperation among Developing Nations,* (TD/B/AC.19/R.8/Add.1., October 1975, p. 21).

An examination of the flow of foreign assistance provided by the fund demonstrates unequivocally that the rate of flow had accelerated very rapidly since 1974. There are many indications based on official publications, as well as on notices to the press, that the rate of lending has been increasing rapidly. For example, the amount of loan commitments in the months of June and July of 1975 was twice as great as the total annual commitments made in the fiscal year of 1973–74. The amount of money committed during those two months of 1975 was almost equal to the total volume of lending during the first decade of operations of the fund.[24]

Undoubtedly, the increase in the rate of lending will have to stabilize itself sometime in the near future. Most probably the stabilized rate will be related to, and will be determined by, the rate of export earnings. The rapid increase in the loan activity that took place in the summer of 1975 was due to several factors that made this increase possible. Some of the factors responsible for this increased flow were: an increase in the authorized capital of the fund, the extension of the eligibility for loans to all developing nations rather than to Arab countries only, and finally also the increased employment of the joint-financing policy with other lending institutions. It may be seen, therefore, that the changes that took place in the summer of 1975 were not only quantitative; they were also qualitative. The fund launched a new policy of co-financing various projects jointly with other Arab organizations. Such a policy, obviously, inaugurated a new trend of closer economic and political cooperation between the Arab countries.

Almost from the very beginning of its existence the Kuwait Fund did not limit its activities to granting loans and to utilizing only its own capital. Obviously, lending its own financial resources has always constituted the major activity of the fund. At the same time, however, the fund extended the field of its activities into a much wider area. One of these areas has been the offer of professional and technical assistance to various countries. This assistance took several forms: preparing feasibility studies, preparing development plans, drafting requests for loans from the I.B.R.D., and assisting in the formulation of plans for educational development. Although this kind of assistance has absorbed only a relatively limited amount of money, nevertheless its effectiveness has been highly successful and has been greatly appreciated.[25] Finally, there has been another aspect of the activities of the fund that proved to be rather successful; namely its activities directed at the promotion of inter-Arab, regional economic cooperation. The Kuwait Fund has been primarily responsible for the launching of the Arab Fund for Economic and Social Development. It presented the idea of forming the AFESD to the Arab Summit meeting in Khartoum in 1967, and when the project was approved by the Arab Summit, the Kuwait Fund provided one-third of its capital and most of its professional staff, and offered also to supply office space for the temporary headquarters of the AFESD.[26]

In addition to sponsoring the formation of the AFESD, the Kuwait Fund also sponsored the establishment of the Inter-Arab Investment Guarantee Corporation.[27] This project, approved by the Council of Arab Economic Unity in Damascus in August of 1970, was aimed at providing Arab private investors a guarantee against losses caused by nationalization, confiscation, and similar types of political, noncommercial risks. In order to further promote the idea of Arab economic cooperation, the fund presented to the Arab League a plan to create an Economic Integration Research Institute. The main function of that Institute would be to conduct economic and industrial studies that would provide basis for closer cooperation and integration between various Arab states. So far, the Institute has not yet been created.

As mentioned earlier, the fund started in 1961 with a rather modest capital of KD 50 million. In 1966 this capital was increased to KD 200 million, and again in 1974 was raised to KD 1 billion (approximately equal to $3.5 billion). According to the amended charter, the fund in addition to using its own capital, is also authorized to borrow funds on the local and international financial markets, equal to five times the amount of its own resources. This opportunity has not been yet utilized by the fund. If, however, the fund decides to fully utilize its capacity to borrow money on the international markets, its total disposable resources would amount to approximately $17.5 billion.

One of the features that characterized the operations of the fund has been its willingness, and frequent eagerness, to cooperate with other financial institutions. Obviously, such an attitude would be highly beneficial to all concerned. The fund believed, quite correctly, that by closely cooperating with other lending institutions operating in essentially the same geographical areas, duplication and incompatibility of various projects could be avoided, and the danger of the debt-service difficulties could be substantially reduced. The fund has also frequently advocated the idea of an annual meeting or an annual review of all major lending institutions in order to harmonize the flow of assistance for various development projects and programs. Although the idea of an annual review has not yet been implemented, nevertheless the Kuwait Fund succeeded in maintaining a very close working relationship with various United Nations Agencies, such as the UNCTAD, DAC, UNIDO, and the UNDP.[28]

Although the field of activities of the KFAED was extended to non-Arab countries in 1974, the first loans to non-Arab countries were actually signed only in the 1975–76 fiscal year, ending June 30, 1976. According to Mr. Fawzi Sultan, the director of the Research Department of the Fund, this delay was unavoidable: "Most of the Third World countries have limited absorptive capacities. The problem is not money, but get a project ready for financing."[29]

This was one of the main reasons why the Kuwait Fund has increasingly turned to cooperation with other Arab regional institutions as well as international bodies such as the World Bank and the UNIDO, as a means of speeding up the flow of foreign assistance to the least-developed nations. It established several joint missions to investigate projects in the potential recipient countries, and it engaged in joint evaluations and joint financing of a project with other Arab or international bodies. During the last fiscal year, for example, the Kuwait Fund has jointly financed eight out of its thirty-four projects.

Loans Provided by the Kuwait Fund, as of December 31, 1976

Country	Number of Loans	Million of KD
Algeria	2	10.0
Bahrain	4	9.3
Egypt	8	51.5
Iraq	2	6.8
Jordan	11	23.5
Lebanon	2	3.4
Mauritania	3	9.4
Morocco	7	23.0
Somalia	2	12.2
Sudan	9	36.7
Syria	3	18.9
Tunisia	11	31.8
Yemen (North)	7	10.8
Yemen (South)	4	9.0
Total	77	246.3

Source: Kuwait Fund for Arab Economic Development, *The Arab World Key Indicators,* May 1977, p. 63–64.

In 1975 the fund decided to change its fiscal year from an April-May schedule to a new schedule covering a period from July 1 to June 30. Thus, the fiscal year 1975–76 actually covers the period of fifteen months: from April 1, 1975 to June 30, 1976.

During that period the fund signed thirty-four new loans for a total of KD 160 million.[30] Twenty of those loans were given to the Arab countries, while the remaining fourteen were allocated to African countries (five loans) and to the non-Arab Asian nations (nine loans). As far as the distribution of the loans to the Arab countries is concerned, they were almost equally divided between agriculture, industry, power, and transportation. Somalia, Sudan, and South Yemen received loans for the development of agriculture. Egypt, Morocco, and Somalia received funds for the development of power stations. There were five loans for the industrial sectors in Egypt, Jordan, Morocco, Sudan, and

Tunisia. Finally, Mauritania, Tunisia, and North Yemen were given loans for the transportation facilities.

In addition to providing loans to various developing nations, the fund also offered fourteen technical assistance grants for KD 2 million, signed four loans totaling KD 12 million to the National Development Banks in Sudan, Morocco, Jordan, and Tunisia, and presented a grant of KD 6 million to the African Development Fund.[31] It may be interesting to note that all loans were granted for projects that were co-financed by other Arab funds or banks.

The loans made during the fiscal year 1975–76 carried an average rate of interest of 4 percent, although some loans granted to North and South Yemen, and to Somalia carried only a 1.5 rate of interest. The repayment period for the loans varied from fifteen to forty years, with the usual five-year grace period.

In attempting to evaluate the operations and the performance of the Kuwait Fund there are several striking features that emerge. From its very inception, the operation of the fund has been very closely identified with the Kuwait government. At the same time the day-to-day functioning of the fund has been characterized by a great deal of informality and a lack of rigid structure. The professional competence of the senior staff has been invariably at the highest level. According to many sources, a significant amount of credit for the successful performance of the fund should be given to its Director-General, Mr. Al-Hamad. He succeeded in maintaining a high-level professional standard of the staff and of the overall functioning of the fund; he also succeeded in cultivating a continuous confidence of the Kuwait government in his leadership, and finally he also managed to channel the loans in such a way that the interest income of the fund has continued to grow at a very encouraging rate.[32]

As far as the lending policies of the fund are concerned, it

Sectoral and Geographical Distribution of Loans
January 1962-June 1976

	Arab Countries		Non-Arab Countries	
	KD Million	Percent	KD Million	Percent
Agriculture	58	24	17	22
Transportation	84	34	6	8
Electricity	53	22	40	54
Industry	52	20	12	16
Total	246	100	75	100

Principal Recipients of Loans
January 1962-June 1976

Countries	Percent
Arab	
Egypt	21
Sudan	14
Tunisia	13
Morocco	9
Syria	8
Jordan	7
Somalia	5
Non-Arab	
India	20
Pakistan	17
Bangladesh	12
Malaysia	10
Sri Lanka	10

Source: Kuwait Fund for Arab Economic
Development, *Annual Report
1975-1976*, pp. 107–10.

can be seen that the fund did not try to adopt a definite formal policy and did not try to follow a rigid pattern in its lending. On the contrary it provided funds for all sorts of projects, usually minor, in all kinds of economic sectors and in all types of countries. It could be also concluded that the effects of those loans, although very significant on the micro-economic level, most probably never reached the macro-economic dimensions.[33]

In addition to directly providing the financial resources for the development of Arab nations, the activities of the fund have also been very successful in providing highly professional, technical, and economic assistance, and secondly, by launching the projects of the AFESD and of the Inter-Arab Investment Guarantee Corporation, the Kuwait Fund has greatly contributed toward the Arab economic collaboration and Arab economic solidarity and unity.[34]

Finally, it should be also emphasized that the Kuwait Fund has actually opened a totally new chapter in the Arab economic relations on the international scene. While at present, there are several national and multinational Arab institutions engaged in lending the surplus petro-dollars to the developing countries, the Kuwait fund has preceded this type of activity by more than a decade. Since the early 1960s it has demonstrated the generosity of the Kuwait government and the Kuwait people in donating a large share of its oil revenue to the less developed Arab nations, and eventually also to the non-Arab countries. The magnitude of this share, in relation to its G.N.P. and to its national budget, has remained unmatched by other Arab nations even in the mid-1970s. It should also be kept in mind that the Kuwait Fund has represented only one channel of the Kuwait foreign aid. Much wider channels of this aid were represented by the direct governmental grants and loans, and also by the flow of private Kuwait investments. Although the size of the flow originating from the Kuwait Fund could be easily ascertained from the official sources and numerous publications, an attempt to measure the total flow of foreign aid from all Kuwait sources would always remain only an estimate.[35]

Notes

1. All data in the introductory section of this chapter are based on: OECD, *Flows of Resources from OPEC Members in Developing Countries* (Paris, 1977).

2. "Aid Programme," *Financial Times Survey,* 25 February 1977, p. 24.

3. "Investment Policy," *Financial Times Survey,* 25 February 1977, p. 22.

4. "Kuwait—Building on a Solid Base," *Financial Times Survey,* 25 February 1977, p. 19.

5. "Investment Policy," *Financial Times Survey.*

6. Ibid.

7. Ibid.

8. Abdlatif Y. Al-Hamad, *Towards a Reassessment of the Recycling Problem* (Kuwait Fund for Arab Economic Development, May 1975), and *Some Aspects of the Oil Controversy* (Kuwait Fund for Arab Economic Development, May 1975).

9. Abdlatif Y. Al-Hamad, *Towards Closer Economic Cooperation in the Middle East* (Kuwait Fund for Arab Economic Development, May 1975), p. 9.

10. Ibrahim F. I. Shihata, *Inter-Arab Equity Joint Ventures* (Kuwait Fund for Arab Economic Development, May 1976).

11. Abdlatif Y. Al-Hamad, *International Finance* (Kuwait Fund for Arab Economic Development, October 1974).

12. Abdlatif Y. Al-Hamad, *Arab Capital Markets* (Kuwait Fund for Arab Economic Development, November 1974).

13. Ibid.

14. Z. A. Nasr, *The Kuwait Fund and Trilateral Cooperation* (Kuwait Fund for Arab Economic Development, February 1977), p. 16.

15. Ibid., p. 17.

16. Ibrahim F. I. Shihata, p. 9.

17. Robert Stephens, *The Arabs' New Frontier* (London: Temple Smith, 1973), p. 44.

18. Abdlatif Y. Al-Hamad, *Arab Capital Markets.*

19. United Nations Conference on Trade and Development, *Financial Cooperation among Developing Nations* (TD/B.AC.19/R.8/Add.1.p.21). Add.1.p.21).

20. Solimar Demir, *The Kuwait Fund and the Political Economy of Arab Regional Development* (New York: Praeger Publishers, 1976), p. 23.

21. Robert Stephens, *The Arabs' New Frontier,* p. 45.

22. Solimar Demir, *The Kuwait Fund,* p. 24.

23. Ibid., p. 47.

24. United Nations Conference on Trade and Development, pp. 18–22.

25. Solimar Demir, *The Kuwait Fund*, p. 56.
26. Robert Stephens, *The Arabs' New Frontier*, p. 67.
27. *The Inter-Arab Investment Guarantee Corporation* (Kuwait Fund for Arab Economic Development, no date).
28. "Aid Programme," *Financial Times Survey*, 25 February 1977, pp. 24–25.
29. Ibid.
30. Kuwait Fund for Arab Economic Development, *Annual Report, 1975/1976*.
31. Ibid.
32. Solimar Demir, *The Kuwait Fund*, p. 32.
33. United Nations Conference on Trade and Development, p. 22.
34. Robert Stephens, *The Arabs' New Frontier*, pp. 70–73.
35. "Investment Policy," *Financial Times Survey*, 25 February 1977, p. 22.

2
Saudi Arabia

Direct Governmental Aid

Since 1974, Saudi Arabia has been one of the largest donors of foreign aid, both in relative terms and also in absolute terms. In relative terms (as percentage of the G.N.P. contributed to foreign aid) Saudi Arabia has been exceeded only by the United Arab Emirates and Kuwait. In absolute terms, only the contributions provided by the United States have been larger than that supplied by Saudi Arabia.

Foreign aid provided by Saudi Arabia to the developing nations has experienced a very rapid change following the increase in the price of oil in 1973. The amount of aid given in 1973 was approximately $335 million.[1] In 1974, however, the volume of Saudi aid increased about five times and equaled approximately $1.6 billion. This was followed by a subsequent increase to $2.5 billion in 1974 and to $2.8 billion in 1975. Since 1974, Saudi Arabia has been on top of the list of the Arab donors of foreign aid. In terms of the percentage of the G.N.P. allocated to foreign assistance, The Saudi aid increased from 4 percent of the G.N.P. in 1973 to slightly more than 7 percent in 1974, 1975, and 1976. During those three years the relative magnitude of the aid has remained essentially stationary.

During the four-year period, 1973–76, a major part of the Saudi aid was of the concessionary type. In 1973 it represented about 90 percent of the total aid, in 1974 it dropped to about 60 percent, and then it increased again in 1975 and 1976 to approximately 80 percent. During this period, about 90 percent of the concessionary aid was of the bilateral character, while only about 10 percent was multinational. Egypt has been the main beneficiary of the Saudi concessional-bilateral aid, usually receiving about 50 percent of that type of aid. Syria, Jordan, and Yemen also received significant volumes of Saudi assistance. In 1976, however, Pakistan received over one-half billion dollars of the concessionary assistance and thus became the largest single recipient.

The composition of the nonconcessionary Saudi aid has remained virtually unchanged over the years. Each year the multilateral type of assistance represented about 90 percent of the total nonconcessionary aid, and invariably the largest share of this type of aid went to the I.B.R.D.

In addition to the concessionary and nonconcessionary aid, Saudi Arabia has also granted the following amounts of credit to the I.M.F. Oil Facility:

$ 654 million in 1974
$1,150 million in 1975
$ 848 million in 1976

An examination of the Saudi aid over the period of 1973–76 would indicate that since 1974 a very definite and steady pattern has emerged. The volume of aid as a percentage of the G.N.P. has remained constant at about 7-percent level, and the division between the concessionary and the nonconcessionary has remained relatively constant, too. Equally unchanged has remained the emphasis on the bilateral form of the concessionary aid, and on the multilateral form of the nonconcessionary assistance.

What has changed, however, is the number and the

character of the recipients. In 1973–74, the aid was limited virtually to three countries (Egypt, Syria, and Jordan), while in 1976 not only the number of countries has increased, but also a substantial part of the assistance has been diverted to countries outside of the Middle East, for example, to Pakistan and Mauritania.

In addition to its very generous contributions to the I.M.F., the Saudi government offered its equally generous assistance to the World Bank (almost $1 billion in 1974) and also to the Islamic Development Bank, to which it subscribed 27 percent of its initial capital.

On the basis of available evidence it could be concluded that most of the financial aid granted to Egypt and Syria was of the program type, while most of the loans granted to other countries were for specific projects. Loans for those projects had to be approved by the Ministry of Finance, while the program financing had to have the approval of the Council of Ministers. In general, it could be stated that a major part of the Saudi foreign assistance had very strong political motivations; over 80 percent of it was granted to the countries directly engaged in confrontation with Israel, namely, Jordan, Egypt, and Syria.

In 1974, the Saudi government, in addition to providing directly aid to various Arab nations, decided to create a special agency, called the Saudi Development Fund. The main purpose behind the formation of this fund was to utilize it as an additional channel for the flow of foreign assistance. Although it was never explicitly stated, the prevailing expectation was that the fund would be primarily used as a channel for foreign aid based on solid economic considerations, while the Saudi government would continue directly to provide financial assistance based on political considerations. Thus, eventually a dual-channel system would be developed, each channel providing a specific type of assistance.

The Saudi Development Fund

The Saudi Development Fund (the S.D.F.) has been formally created on September 1, 1974, by the Council of Ministers and approved by the king. It started its operations in the early part of 1975.[2]

According to the charter of the S.D.F., the fund shall participate in the financing of various development projects in the developing countries, through granting loans (article 1 of the charter). The capital of the fund was fixed at SR 10 billion (approximately $2.8 billion). The fund was authorized to lend out 50 percent of its capital during the first three years of its operations. The capital of the fund could be, however, increased by a decision of the Council of Ministers. According to article 3 of the charter, the fund is administered by the board of directors, chaired by the Minister of Finance and National Economy. The board of directors consists of a vice-chairman who is also the managing director of the fund and is appointed by the Council of Ministers, and four other members who are experts in the areas of finance and economics. They are appointed for a period of three years. The main function of the board of directors is to administer the fund. Specifically, it should decide on the conditions of each loan, it should determine how the revenues of the fund should be invested, and finally, it should approve the administrative and financial by-laws of the fund.

Article 6 of the charter requests the board of directors, prior to approving an application for a loan, to conduct a feasibility study of the project, to analyze the general economic situation of the prospective borrower and to study the availability of other sources used in co-financing of the projects. The lending policies of the fund were very explicitly defined by its charter. It provided, among others, that the amount of each loan shall not exceed 5 percent of the fund's capital and shall be limited to no more than 50 percent of the total cost of the project. Furthermore, the total amount of money lent to any one country shall not exceed 10 percent of the fund's capital. The borrowing country, according to the charter, was required to submit a proper report at frequent intervals to the board of directors, and it should also facilitate any inspections that the fund may consider necessary. The fund started its operation in March 1975, and H. E. Mohammed Aba al-Khail was appointed as the chairman of the fund, while Dr. Mahsoun B. Jabal assumed the position of the vice-chairman and managing director. At the end of the first fiscal year (June 30, 1975) the S.D.F. had granted four loans for a total of SR 483 million and made commitments for an additional fifteen loans, equal to SR 1.24 billion.

The loans granted in the first fiscal year included a loan of SR 175 million to Egypt, SR 105 million to Tunisia, SR 105 million to Uganda, and SR 98 million to Sudan. The projects covered by those loans included repairs to the Suez Canal, an irrigation project, and agricultural development plan. The loans committed during those first few months of operations of the S.D.F. included four loans to Egypt for approximately SR 450 million, five loans to Mali for approximately SR 105 million, four loans to Malaysia for approximately SR 250 million, and two loans to Indonesia for about SR 400 million. As far as the distribution of all loans granted and committed was concerned, it was channeled to infrastructure (45 percent), agriculture (41 percent), and health and education (14 percent).

During the second half of 1975 and early 1976 (the second fiscal year of the S.D.F.), the fund has approved a total of ten loans representing an amount of SR 995 million. The two largest recipients of loans were Egypt (SR 400 million) and Malaysia (SR 270 million). The proceeds of the loans to Egypt were directed toward the rebuilding of the Suez

Canal, while the loans to Malaysia were divided almost equally between agriculture and education.

The activities of the fund increased very substantially during the third fiscal year of its operations, starting in July 1976. During that fiscal year the fund granted twenty-two loans for a total of SR 1.55 billion. The largest recipients of the loans were Egypt, Mali, Pakistan, and Indonesia. The year 1976 marked also a beginning of a new trend in the lending policies of the fund. Although the bulk of the loans was still concentrated in Arab or Muslim countries, for the first time the fund extended some of its loans to non-Muslim countries, such as, for example, South Korea, Rwanda, Congo, and China (Taiwan).

In the early part of 1977, the S.D.F. was in the process of finalizing loans to twenty-seven countries in Africa and Asia, and also for the first time, in South America. Two loans to Brazil and Ecuador, totaling SR 277 million, for electric power stations were under consideration. The largest recipients of loans were, however, located in Asia: India, Bangladesh, Indonesia, and Malaysia received the largest loans from the fund.

In reviewing the operations of the S.D.F. since the start of its operations in March 1975 until July 1976, several conclusions could be formulated. Not counting the commitments for loans but considering only the loans actually signed, the fund had granted SR 4.6 billion in loans to twenty-three countries for over fifty various projects. Seventy-one percent of the loans were directed to infrastructure, 18 percent to agriculture, and 11 percent to health and education. The continent of Asia received 52 percent of the loans, Africa 45 percent, and other continents 3 percent.

On the average, a typical loan was granted for a period of twenty years, carried an interest rate of between 2 to 3 percent, and a grace period of 5 years. In most cases the loans covered approximately 15 percent of the total cost of the project, and the projects concerned would be completed over a period of 4 to 5 years.

If, in addition to the loans actually signed, the loan commitments are considered also, the magnitude of the operations of the S.D.F. would increase very substantially. During the period of slightly more than two years (March 1975–July 1977), the fund has either signed or committed itself to over seventy loans, equal to over SR 7 billion (about $2 billion). The scale of the operations of the S.D.F. has been very impressive from several points of view. First of all, the amount of money involved, almost one billion dollars annually, represents a striking example of the generosity of the Saudi government. Secondly, it is equally remarkable that the fund was able to reach such a scale of activities almost immediately after its official formation. Finally, it may be noted that the fund proved to be much more successful than many experts were anticipating in the early part of 1975. Frequently, many apprehensions were expressed that the S.D.F. will be confronted with a very serious shortage of professional staff and that this shortage will slow down the processing and the evaluation of the applications for loans. Fortunately, most of those fears proved to be unjustified, and the S.D.F. managed from its very beginning to launch a very successful flow of assistance for economic development in various parts of Asia and Africa. Considering the number of loans that were in the processing stage in the second half of 1977, it may be safely assumed that the scale of operations that was so successfully reached in the past will also be maintained in the future years.

Notes

1. All data in this section are based on OECD, *Flows of Resources from OPEC Members to Developing Countries* (Paris, 1977); United Nations Conference on Trade and Development, *Financial Co-operation among Developing Countries* (TD/B/AC.19/R.8) and (TD/B/AC.19/R.8/Add.1), 29 October 1975; *International Financial Co-operation for Development* (TD/188/Supp.1./Add.a.), 20 February 1976; *Elements of a Program of Economic Co-operation among Developing Countries* (TD/192/Supp.1), 26 March 1976.

2. All information concerning the activities of the Saudi Fund for Development are based on The Saudi Fund for Development, *First Annual Report* and *Annual Report 1975/76*.

3
United Arab Emirates

The foreign aid supplied by the U.A.E. has consistently remained at a very high level, both in absolute terms and also in relative terms, with reference to the G.N.P. Since 1974, the U.A.E. has continuously occupied the position of the third largest donor of foreign aid (in terms of dollars) among the Arab countries, being surpassed only by Saudi Arabia and Kuwait.

In relative terms, expressed as percentage of the G.N.P. given in foreign aid, the Emirates have occupied second place, being surpassed only by Qatar in 1973 and 1975, and by Kuwait in 1974 and 1976. Throughout this period, the percentage of the G.N.P. given away as foreign aid varied from about 10 percent to more than 13 percent, while the volume has reached the level of $1.2 billion in 1975 and 1976.[1]

What makes those figures even more remarkable and more astonishing is the fact that the economic advancement of the Emirates during the 1960s was at a level well below that of other Arab oil-exporting countries, and furthermore, the Emirates became a political entity only in December 1971. In spite of that, the U.A.E. has succeeded in attaining a leading position among the Arab states as far as the generosity in giving aid is concerned.

There are several distinct features that characterize the foreign aid provided by the U.A.E.[2] The volume of concessionary aid very definitely dominated the flow of the non-concessionary assistance. In 1973 all aid was of the concessionary character, while in 1974, 1975, and 1976 the concessionary type of aid represented about 90 percent of the total aid. Furthermore, over 90 percent of the concessionary aid was of the bilateral character and almost all of it was directed to three countries, Egypt, Jordan, and Syria.

The nonconcessionary aid decreased from $239 million in 1974 to $122 million in 1976, and over this three-year period was more or less evenly divided between the bilateral and multilateral. Yugoslavia, Spain, and Congo were among the recipients of the bilateral, nonconcessionary aid. The overall picture that emerges from an examination of the volume and the directions of the foreign aid provided by the U.A.E. is a very clear one indeed; the magnitude of aid has been continuously at a very high level, and the bulk of it has gone to Egypt, Syria, and Jordan. It may be concluded, therefore, that the political considerations very definitely dominated the character of the Emirates' assistance to foreign nations.

The preceding section presented an overall picture of the foreign aid programs for the whole country of the United Arab Emirates. The discussion that follows will concentrate on Abu Dhabi, which constitutes the most important part of the federation of the U.A.E. Although the exact figures are not always readily available, it is generally estimated that Abu Dhabi accounts for approximately 90 percent of the population, the G.N.P., production of oil, and of the national budget of the whole federation of the U.A.E.

The policy of the government of Abu Dhabi, with respect to foreign aid, represents a very striking and unusual picture. The country itself entered the international political area only in the 1970s. It has a very small indigenous population that is approaching a quarter of a million inhabitants. At least 75 percent of the labor force consists of foreigners; most of them are illegal immigrants from Pakistan, Iran, Afghanistan, and Oman.[3] The economy of the country is based on one commodity only, oil. In 1975 the production of oil amounted to 1.7 million barrels per day, and it increased in 1976 to 2 million per day. However, according to many estimates, the volume of production is kept artificially low, and could be very easily increased by about 50 percent.[4]

In spite of its small population and its natural resources being limited to one commodity only, the government of Abu Dhabi has been allocating a larger portion of its G.N.P. to foreign aid than any other country in the world. In 1975, it allocated close to one billion dollars and in 1976 the flow of aid increased to $1.25 billion.[5] In terms of percentages of the G.N.P. Abu Dhabi allocated close to 30 percent of its G.N.P. in 1976 to foreign aid. This figure compares with less than one-half percent for the OECD countries and with about 6 percent for the OPEC countries. According to a recent study conducted by the *Financial Times* (London), "In the past five years of its existence no less than 20 percent of Abu Dhabi oil revenues have been disbursed in aid—not counting extra-budget handouts to neighboring Rulers."[6] Furthermore, "an extraordinary high proportion has been in the form of outright grants, particularly to the 'confrontation' states."[7]

This extremely high proportion of the G.N.P. allocated to foreign assistance can be explained essentially by two factors. First, purely on humanitarian grounds, the government of Abu Dhabi has been firmly dedicated to share its sudden and unexpected wealth with less fortunate nations. Such a policy was unequivocally proclaimed by the president of the U.A.E., Shaikh Zayed ibn Sultan Al Nahayan. At the time when he was assuming office, he proclaimed that "this wealth is not for us alone; it must be shared, and, furthermore, such aid will be an investment for our country."[8]

This view has been also confirmed by the Minister of

Petroleum and Mineral Resources, Dr. Mana Al Otaiba, when he said that "no country, no matter how secluded can hope to exist prosperously for long when its neighbors are poor."[9]

The second reason that could probably account for this extremely high ratio between foreign aid and the G.N.P. is simply the fact that the absorptive capacity of the local economy is very limited and in spite of strenuous efforts by the government, the country simply cannot spend any more money than it has been actually spending.[10] In 1976, for example, after very generous spending on the local economy, and after equally generous contributions to the Abu Dhabi Fund for Arab Economic Development, and to the other Arab development funds, the government of Abu Dhabi was left with a surplus of over one billion dollars that had to be invested somewhere.[11] To take care of such surpluses, the government established in March 1976 the Abu Dhabi Investment Authority. This agency, in cooperation with several leading European and American banks, will serve as a channel for investing the surplus funds on Wall Street and on various European stock exchanges.[12] It is estimated that between March 1976 and February 1977, this agency has invested over one billion dollars. In addition to placing a significant volume of liquid funds on various stock markets in Europe and in the U.S., the government of Abu Dhabi has also purchased various real-estate properties in Europe, and also has very generously contributed to various organizations, such as the P.L.O.[13]

The absorptive capacity is limited not only within the economy of Abu Dhabi, but it exists, also, and probably on an even larger scale, for the economy of the whole federation of the United Arab Emirates. For example, in the 1976 and 1977 fiscal years, the government of the U.A.E. was able to spend only 30 percent of its approved budget. The remaining 70 percent was simply left unspent.

In spite of the general knowledge that the government of Abu Dhabi, as well as the government of the United Arab

Emirates, contributes heavily to various programs of foreign assistance and at the same time it rapidly increases its investments in foreign countries, it is impossible to ascertain exactly the dividing line between foreign investments and foreign aid. Although the government is providing some information on this subject, nevertheless, many governmental decisions and policies are confidential and are not publicized. Furthermore, until very recently the dividing line between the public revenue of the government and the private revenue of the ruler was not very clearly defined. Even today, in the state of Dubai the oil revenue accruing to that country is still considered as a private income of the ruler, Shekh Rashid. In spite of this lack of complete and accurate data, there is enough evidence available to support the claims of the government that in the fiscal year of 1977 it expected to allocate about 30 percent of the G.N.P. on foreign aid. This would indicate an increase from 25 percent in 1975, from 27 percent in 1976, and from 20 percent in 1974.[14]

An attempt to project the magnitude of the foreign aid into the future would most likely indicate that this rate of increase will not be maintained. On the one hand, the oil revenues of Abu Dhabi are most likely to level off, while at the same time the absorptive capacity of the local economy and the availability of local investment opportunities will increase. It may be expected, therefore, that the figure of 30 percent may indicate the peak of spending on foreign aid by Abu Dhabi, and most probably also by any other country. Any projection of future foreign aid from Abu Dhabi is further complicated by the fact that in 1977 that country has experienced, rather suddenly and unexpectedly, a mild financial crisis and a rather serious real-estate crash. Apparently the local real-estate market found itself with a large surplus of vacant buildings, especially of office type, and several leading local banks were confronted with bankruptcy. The government reacted in a very decisive way, and largely succeeded in preventing the local real-estate and banking crash to spread to other parts of the economy.[15] During that crisis, the pillar of the economic structure, the oil sector, has remained unaffected. It can be assumed, therefore, that a continuous flow of oil revenues will also assure the continuation of the flows of foreign aid. At the same time, it should not be expected that the volume of foreign assistance will exceed its present level of 30 percent of the G.N.P. An examination of the balance of payments and the balance of trade of the U.A.E., to which Abu Dhabi contributes over 90 percent, would very strongly indicate a leveling-off trend. The net foreign trade balance of the U.A.E. was equal to $5.5 billion in 1974. It decreased to $4.5 billion in 1975 and it increased slightly in 1976 to $5.2 billion.[16] As long as the production of oil will remain at its present level of about 2 million barrels a day, and as long as the propensity to import will continue its slow increase, one could not expect that the magnitude of the funds available for foreign aid would increase. On the contrary, it seems that it may show a gradual decline in the immediate future.

The Abu Dhabi Fund for Arab Economic Development

The Abu Dhabi Fund for Arab Economic Development was established on a rather modest scale in 1971, with an initial capital of approximately $12 million. Until 1974 the fund had remained relatively inactive. The volume of its activities increased very rapidly in 1974, when the capital was increased to $500 million and the scope of its activities was extended to all developing countries, rather than limited to Arab nations only, as the name of the fund seemed to imply. In addition to utilizing its own capital, the fund has also been authorized to borrow an amount equal to twice its subscribed capital. In spite of the official extension of the geographical scope of the fund, almost all of its financial assistance has been channeled to Arab countries. In 1974 the fund provided a total of about $60 million in loans. The major loans were granted to Bahrain ($10 million), Egypt ($15 million), Jordan ($6 million), Mauritania ($4 million), Somalia ($7 million), Syria ($11 million), and Tunisia ($6 million).[17] In 1975 the major loans were given to Jordan ($70 million), Egypt ($32 million), and Syria ($24 million). During the eighteen-month period covering 1974–75, Egypt and Jordan were the largest recipients of assistance provided by the fund. Those countries received about two-thirds of all aid supplied by the fund.

The fund increased the volume of its activities very substantially in 1976.[18] New loans granted during that year amounted to approximately $165 million, as compared to about $150 million granted during the preceding two-year period. In 1976, seventeen new loans were granted. Over 40 percent of the proceeds of the loans was allocated for the development of the industrial sector, while about 35 percent was directed for the development of the electrical power. It can be seen, therefore, that over three-fourths of the aid provided by the fund was directed to the industrial and energy sectors. The funds allocated to agriculture accounted for about 20 percent only. The distribution of funds in 1976 among various sectors follows essentially the same pattern adopted in 1974 and 1975. The total amount of assistance provided by the fund in 1974, 1975, and 1976 was over $270 million.

In 1976 the fund started following a new policy as far as the geographical distribution of its assistance was concerned. Prior to that year, all aid was directed to the Arab countries only. In 1976, only 75 percent of aid was allocated to the Arab countries while the remaining 25 percent was directed to the non-Arab nations in Asia and Africa. At the same time, the fund initiated a large number of feasibility studies for various industrial projects in Africa. It was anticipated that in 1977 more than 50 percent of the assistance would be channeled to the non-Arab countries in Africa and Asia. Some of the largest projects under consideration for 1977 included:

$75 million for an electric power network in Indonesia,
$65 million for sugar refineries in Tanzania,
$65 million for sugar plantations in Afghanistan,
$48 million for railway network in Tunisia, and
$18 million for a hydroelectric facility in Senegal.

Some of the largest single projects financed by the fund in 1976[19] included:

$25 million for electric power stations in Bahrain,
$24 million for a cotton textile mill in Sudan,
$20 million for a textile mill in Morocco,
$15 million for surveys of oil fields in Oman,
$18 million for power stations in India, and
$10 million for a tool factory in Bangladesh.

The majority of loans granted in 1976 was for a period of twelve to twenty years, with a usual grace period of four to six years, and the rate of interest varied from 3 percent to 4.5 percent. Almost all of the projects in which the fund participated were also co-financed by various multinational financial organizations. An examination of the financial operations of the Abu Dhabi Fund during the 1974–76 period reveals several very striking features.[20] According to the data presented by the fund, it appears that the fund concentrated almost exclusively on project loans and avoided any commitments to program lending. Furthermore, it also appears that in granting loans the fund was motivated primarily by the commercial considerations, while the political considerations or the general situation of the balance of payment of the recipient country played a very minor role, if any, in deciding on the merits of a specific loan. In addition to granting loans from its own resources, the fund was also authorized to participate in equity financing and in guaranteeing loans granted by other lenders. The fund's participation in equity financing projects was limited to 15 percent of the total equity of a project. In general, the fund has shown no specific preference concerning the economic sectors for its lending; as mentioned above, the main consideration in approving a loan was placed on the profitability of the project involved. As a general rule, the fund considered a rate of return of 15 percent as a minimum that would justify a commitment of its funds to a prospective borrower.

In analyzing and comparing the foreign aid policies of the Abu Dhabi government and of the Abu Dhabi Fund, one can immediately detect a very clear-cut dividing line between the policies of those two bodies. The government adopted a policy of great generosity by providing funds for program support, for balance of payments support, and various political and social causes of the Arab world. The fund, on the other hand, followed a completely different policy. It concentrated its lending almost exclusively on specific projects, and in approving loans, it consistently applied very strict commercial considerations. In effect, the fund actually operated more like a commercial banking institution than as a source of foreign assistance.

In late 1976, the government of Abu Dhabi indicated that the fund would extend its activities to areas outside of the Arab world and undertake the financing of several large-scale projects in India, Sri Lanka, Burundi, Mali, and Indonesia.[21] At the same time, the fund was becoming increasingly aware that the main problem facing it in those countries would be the shortage of trained personnel who could be engaged in the identification and evaluation of potential projects, and in preparing feasibility studies. In discussing the problem facing the fund in the immediate future, the director of the fund, Mr. Al-Muwais, stated that "the problem with the poorest countries is not finding money, but identifying and evaluating projects."[22] To overcome this difficulty, he suggested that close cooperation with various United Nations agencies and collaboration with economic experts provided by the U.N. would greatly enhance the efficiency of the operations of the fund. In late 1976 and early 1977, the management of the fund launched a definite program of securing closer working relations with the UNDP, and also with the development funds of the neighboring Arab states.[23] In 1977, a series of meetings took place between the directors of the Abu Dhabi Fund and the executives of the funds in Kuwait and Saudi Arabia. It may be interesting to note that the Abu Dhabi Fund, starting in 1976, very definitely decided to adopt a policy of close cooperation and collaboration with similar institutions in other Arab countries.[24]

At the same time as the directors of the fund announced their new policy of expanding the activities of the fund to areas outside of the Arab world, the charter of the fund was modified so that the fund could assume several functions usually performed by a commercial banking institution. The revised charter allowed the fund to accept deposits from the local public corporations and it also allowed it to participate actively in organizing various financial institutions on the domestic scene. It is too early yet to obtain conclusive evidence that would indicate to what extent the fund has shifted its attention from the foreign scene to the domestic scene. There is, however, some evidence available that would strongly suggest that during the financial and banking crisis that Abu Dhabi experienced in 1977, the fund played a significant role in rescuing some of the local banks from bankruptcy.[25] If this trend of increasing involvement in domestic financial affairs continues, it would seem that the role of the fund as a source of foreign assistance flowing to the underdeveloped nations would gradually decrease. It is also probable that in such a case the function of providing foreign aid would gradually move directly into the hands of the government.

Only after the publication of the annual report for 1977 would it be possible to ascertain to what extent the fund was successful in widening the area of its activities to the African continent and to Southeast Asia, and to what extent the financial crisis at home forced it to play an increasingly active role on the domestic scene.

Notes

1. O.E.C.D., *Flows of Resources from OPEC Members to Developing Countries* (Paris, 1977).
2. Ibid.
3. "United Arab Emirates," *Financial Times Survey* (London), 8 June 1977, p. 15.
4. "Oil," *Financial Times Survey* (London), 8 June 1977, p. 18.
5. "The Economy," *Financial Times Survey* (London), 8 June 1977, p. 16.
6. "United Arab Emirates," p. 15.
7. Ibid.
8. "Five Years of the United Arab Emirates," *International Herald Tribune*, 1 December 1976, p. 8.
9. Ibid.
10. "Focus: United Arab Emirates," A Special Report, *International Herald Tribune*, November 1977, p. 1.
11. "The Economy."
12. "Generous Foreign Aid Programme," *Financial Times Survey* (London), 11 February 1977, p. 23.
13. "United Arab Emirates," p. 15.
14. "Abu Dhabi," *The Economist*, 4 December 1976, p. 78; "Focus: United Arab Emirates."
15. "Abu Dhabi," *Financial Times Survey* (London), 8 June 1977, p. 21.

16. "Abu Dhabi," *The Economist,* 4 December 1976, p. 78.
17. Abu Dhabi Fund for Arab Economic Development, *Annual Report, 1976,* p. 16.
18. Ibid., pp. 20–21.
19. Ibid., p. 24.
20. Ibid., p. 53 ff.
21. "Abu Dhabi," *The Economist.*
22. "Generous Foreign Aid Programme," *Financial Times Survey.*
23. The United Arab Emirates," *The Guardian* (U.K.), 14 December 1976, pp. 23 ff.
24. A.D.F.A.E.D., *Annual Report, 1976,* p. 21.
25. "Property," *Financial Times Survey* (London), 8 June 1977, p. 30.

4
Iraq, Libya, and Qatar

Iraq, Libya, and Qatar are grouped together in this study simply because their role in providing foreign aid is rapidly diminishing. The volume of their aggregate assistance has been decreasing both in terms of dollars and also in relation to the magnitude of the aid provided by other Arab countries, namely, Saudi Arabia, Kuwait, and the United Arab Emirates.

The combined aid of Iraq, Libya, and Qatar reached its peak in 1974 and 1975, at a level approaching one billion dollars annually.[1] In 1976 it declined to approximately $700 million. The same declining trend has been shown in relation to the aid provided by the other Arab nations. In 1973 the combined aid of Iraq, Libya, and Qatar represented about one-third of the total Arab assistance. In 1974 this share declined to one-fourth, in 1975 to less than one-fifth, and in 1976 to slightly more than one-tenth.

Iraq

The flow of assistance from Iraq seems to be following a very definite declining trend, both in absolute and in relative terms. The volume of foreign assistance decreased from $440 million in 1974 to $250 million in 1975 and to $120 million in 1976. At the same time, the volume of aid in relative terms, expressed as a percentage of the G.N.P. offered in aid has declined from 4.16 percent in 1974 to 1.9 percent in 1975, and to 0.75 percent in 1976. Usually, approximately 90 percent of the foreign aid was of the bilateral, concessionary type, with Egypt, Syria, and Lebanon being the principal receiving countries. This rapidly declining flow of foreign aid seems to be indicating that soon the flow may stop altogether. Furthermore, any conclusions derived from the examination of the volume and of the directions of the Iraqi foreign aid should be considered as very tentative and should be approached with caution. According to the United Nations and the OECD sources, while the data provided by the Iraq government in 1973 and 1974 may have a certain degree of certainty and reliability, they are definitely incomplete, and not very reliable, as far as the years of 1975 and 1976 are concerned. It is generally believed that the volume of aid actually provided was significantly higher than the figures presented by the Iraq government would seem to indicate. Nevertheless, the government of Iraq, for reasons known only to itself, preferred to consider the foreign aid data as confidential.

The flow of economic assistance provided by Iraq is channeled through a multitude of various governmental institutions. A major part of it is granted by the Central Bank and by the Ministry of Finance, while smaller amounts are distributed by other ministries and various state agencies, including the recently created Iraqi Fund for Foreign Development. As there is no centralized and all-inclusive source of information that would include all channels of foreign aid, it is impossible to present a comprehensive summary of the Iraqi foreign aid. Several attempts have been made by the United Nations agencies to estimate the total volume of the flow of foreign aid. It is believed, however, that a detailed summary based on the available information accounts for only about 50 percent of the economic assistance. The remaining 50 percent is granted by various governmental agencies without any public announcements.

It is estimated that in 1974 Iraq offered close to one billion dollars in foreign aid. The officially published commitments account for only $447 million. An additional $160 million was committed by the Iraqi government to the Iraqi Fund for Foreign Development. However, no detailed information has been presented that would account for the allocation of this sum. Furthermore, additional sums of money were contributed to various United Nations agencies, but again no details were officially announced. On the basis of the limited available data, it can be estimated that the magnitude of the flow of foreign assistance in 1975 was essentially similar to the flow in 1974.

In general, it may be concluded that Iraq has not adopted a definite policy or a definite system of priorities as far as its foreign aid is concerned. It appears that most grants were given to those countries with which Iraq has special relations or maintains special interests, and the decisions concerning the grants were based on a case-by-case basis. The most frequent form of aid was a grant of a certain quantity of oil. Another form also frequently adopted was a loan for a specific project.

The main reason that accounts for a lack of a systematic and comprehensive policy toward foreign assistance is the fact that Iraq basically is not a surplus country, and furthermore, Iraq itself has great needs for its own economic development. At the same time, Iraq lacks a body of professional manpower that could examine and evaluate the requests for foreign aid. For that reason, very frequently the political aspects of a loan seemed to be more important than purely economic considerations. This fact accounts also to a large extent for the failure to formulate a long-range policy for channeling foreign assistance.

In the past, the Iraqi government has shown a definite preference for concentrating its foreign assistance on bilateral arrangements rather than on multilaterial institutions. In most cases, granting of a loan on a bilateral basis involved formation of a joint venture with the recipient country. In general, the Iraqi government has adopted in the past a rather passive attitude toward its program of foreign aid. Most requests for loans have been generated by the recipient countries, and the Iraqi government has not created an institutional framework for identification or for evaluation of potential projects. The government believed that the most efficient form of distributing the assistance funds was by direct contacts between the Iraqi government agencies and the recipient countries. This policy has apparently been modified to a certain extent in 1974, when the government has officially created the Iraqi Fund for Foreign Development (I.F.F.D.). Nevertheless, throughout 1975 and 1976 this fund has remained totally inactive. An allocation of $168 million was made to the fund in 1975; so far, however, no official disbursement from the fund has been made. Only an announcement that money has been received by the Fund was made by the Ministry of Finance. The constitution of the Iraqi Fund for Foreign Development provides that the fund should concentrate its activities on Arab countries and should give priority to those projects that would contribute to closer economic cooperation and integration between the Arab countries. Officially, the fund should operate as an independent governmental agency, governed by a board of directors appointed by the president of Iraq for a period of three years. As mentioned previously, however, the fund has remained so far inactive. At the moment, it would be rather difficult to predict whether the fund eventually will start its operations, or whether it will gradually disappear. Considering the fact that Iraq's needs for financing its own development are rapidly increasing and there is therefore no chance for an accumulation of a substantial surplus on the balance of payments, it may be expected that the second alternative is more likely to take place.

Libya

The flow of foreign aid originating from Libya shows a pattern that is different from that of all other Arab nations offering foreign assistance, except Iraq.

While all other Arab countries have increased the volume of their aid and also the share of aid in their G.N.P.s during the 1973–76 period, Libya has indicated a trend in the opposite direction. The size of aid in terms of dollars has shown a slight decrease (from $400 million to $370 million), and the percentage of the G.N.P. donated in aid has dropped from 6.25 percent to 2.43 percent.

The division of aid between concessionary and the nonconcessionary has changed also. In 1973–75 more aid was of the concessionary type, while in 1976 the nonconcessionary aid became more than twice as large as the concessionary type. In all instances, however, the bilateral assistance was larger than the multilateral, and the number of the receiving countries was rather large, while the list of the receiving countries varied significantly from year to year. It may be interesting to note that in 1974 Libya provided aid to Argentina and in 1976 to Spain and Portugal. Libya, therefore, has been probably the only African country supplying economic assistance to Latin America and Europe.

The declining volume of aid, both in absolute and in relative terms, would seem to indicate that Libya may be losing interest in these types of activities. At the same time it would be rather difficult to offer a satisfactory explanation for the rapidly changing list of recipient countries, and for the shifts from concessionary aid to nonconcessionary.

Most probably those changes reflect more the personal preferences of the Libyan leaders rather than a major shift in political or economic considerations.

The available data concerning the flow of foreign aid from Libya are very far from being complete or reliable. There is no single agency within the Libyan government that would be responsible for granting foreign assistance or for collecting the information about foreign aid and presenting it to the public in general or to the news media.

Furthermore, the Libyan government has never formally announced its policy concerning foreign aid. No long-range objectives were ever declared and no formal criteria for the evaluation of the requests for aid have ever been presented. It appears that the decisions concerning the flow of foreign aid are based on ad hoc basis, and are influenced as much by political considerations as by purely economic ones. There is, however, one feature that seems to dominate the flow of Libyan foreign aid. The available data clearly indicate a very wide geographical distribution of aid. The number of countries receiving aid has been rather large while the size of each individual loan has been rather modest. Libya has granted numerous loans to the sub-Saharan African countries, to several Latin American nations, and also to Spain, Portugal, and Turkey. The largest single recipient of aid has been Egypt; in 1973 Libya announced a grant of almost one billion dollars to Egypt, and almost $200 million were actually disbursed at that time. Libya has also contributed to a large number of various multilateral institutions. The Islamic Development Bank and the Arab Bank for Economic Development of Africa have been the two largest recipients of funds. In general, according to the available information, it appears rather clearly that the Libyan government has shown a definite preference for providing funds to the multilateral agencies rather than providing aid on bilateral basis.

The nonconcessional flows of money from Libya were

largely concentrated on the Arab countries and on Pakistan. In most cases they took form of joint ventures in the areas of banking, investment houses, holding companies, and similar institutions. Most of those flows were directed by the Libyan Arab Foreign Bank and the National Investment Company.

The Libyan Arab Foreign Bank was established in 1972 with a capital of $60 million. It is owned by the Libyan government, and its main function is to engage in banking and financial activities outside of Libya. In 1973 and 1974, the bank provided development loans to Algeria, Egypt, Tunisia, and Uganda. It also established joint branch banks in Abu Dhabi, Chad, Lebanon, Spain, Togo, and Somalia. The bank, either directly or indirectly through the joint branch banks established in foreign countries, provided funds for specific projects. The economic evaluation of the prospective projects has usually been undertaken by the bank itself or by various agencies of the United Nations. Throughout its whole existence the bank has always cooperated very closely with the United Nations agencies and has relied on its professional manpower. It appears also that in most cases the primary criteria for granting loans by the bank was the economic feasibility of a specific project rather than the development picture of the recipient country as a whole.

The National Investment Company was formed in 1972 with an initial capital of $12.2 million. Its main function was to provide financial services, on strictly commercial bases, both inside and outside of Libya. So far, most of the activities of the National Investment Company have been concentrated on the development of tourist facilities in Mediterranean countries. Tunisia, Lebanon, and Malta have been the largest recipients of the investments funds from N.I.Co. The usual form of operation of N.I.Co. was to form a company, jointly owned by N.I.Co. and some local investors. It has to be emphasized that all activities of N.I.Co. were based on strictly commercial considerations. On several occasions N.I.Co. participated also in joint projects with various European financial groups, especially French and Italian.

In conclusion, there are two aspects of the Libyan foreign aid that ought to be emphasized. First, as the flow of assistance is channeled through numerous agencies and institutions, it is rather difficult to present a comprehensive picture of the total flow. Secondly, it appears that there exists a wide gap between the officially announced commitments and the actual disbursements of the assistance funds. This gap magnifies, of course, the difficulties in attempting to present a clear and accurate picture of Libyan foreign assistance. As far as future trends of the volume of capital flow for foreign assistance are concerned, it could be stated that all indications seem to point toward an increased volume. The capacity of the Libyan economy to absorb larger volumes of investments seems to be rather limited, while on the other hand, the earnings generated by oil exports will most likely continue to grow. Thus, the available funds for foreign assistance will most likely continue to increase also. The case of Libya is in all probability very similar to the case of Saudi Arabia and Kuwait; in the foreseeable future those three countries will continue to generate a surplus on their respective balances of payments, and will continue therefore to be the main sources of Arab foreign aid.

Qatar

Qatar, one of the smallest states on the Arabian Gulf that gained its full independence only in 1971, has one of the highest percentages of its G.N.P. allocated to foreign assistance. Unfortunately, there is a lack of statistical data that would provide a complete and detailed analysis of the flows of foreign aid offered by Qatar. As there are no special institutions dealing with the distribution and allocation of foreign aid, the funds are provided directly by the government, usually by the Ministry of Finance.

In 1973 the total volume of concessionary and nonconcessionary aid amounted to approximately 22 percent of the G.N.P., and in 1974 it dropped to about 17 percent, although the volume in terms of dollars increased from $134 million in 1973 to $345 million in 1974, and to $367 million in 1975. When it is recognized that the native population of Qatar is approximately 20,000, it can be easily concluded that Qatar has the highest ratio of foreign aid to the G.N.P. per capita in the world.

The flow of foreign aid from Qatar started only in 1973, almost all of it was directed to Egypt, Jordan, and Syria. Those three countries received about $100 million. Relatively small amounts were also allocated to Yemen and Oman. In 1974, Qatar extended the geographical coverage of its aid, and in addition to the usual recipients (Egypt, Jordan, and Syria), significant aid was directed to Arab countries in Africa (Somalia, Sudan, Morocco, Tunisia, and Mauritania). Outside of Africa, Pakistan was the most significant recipient of Qatar's aid in 1974 and 1975. Although most of the aid to the African countries was officially classified as development loans for specific projects, from the practical point of view, those loans actually had the character of grants for general development, because Qatar had no qualified personnel and no opportunity to evaluate the feasibility studies on the basis of which those development loans were granted.

In addition to the concessionary assistance, Qatar provided also some nonconcessionary aid, directed almost exclusively to Egypt. In 1973 it amounted to $20 million and in 1974 to approximately $80 million.

The allocations of foreign assistance, especially in 1974 and 1975, showed a rather wide geographical distribution, with relatively large amounts going to Morocco and Mauritania, and relatively smaller amounts to the central African countries of Chad and Mali. It seems very likely that Qatar has not yet formulated a definite policy concerning the allocation of its aid; most likely the allocation of loans and grants was influenced more by the political events of the day rather than by long-range economic objectives. It is very probable that the government of Qatar has been attempting to obtain a maximum of political good will from its foreign aid program. At the same time, the supply of funds from Qatar's budget has been most likely determined by the capacity of the local economy to absorb the flow of investment funds. For example, in 1976 the national budget provided for about $2 billion of revenues, almost entirely from the export of oil, while at the same time, it could identify only about one billion dollars of expenditure items. It is rather obvious that Qatar's economy, in spite of a very rapid rate of economic progress, and in spite of a relatively substantial accomplishment in the development of the industrial base and of the social infrastructure, has a rather limited capacity to absorb more investment funds in the forseeable future. The shortage of labor and the small population base prevent a higher rate of absorption. The total population of Qatar, concentrated mostly in the urban area of Doha, amounts to only 200,000, while the native-born population represents only about 10 percent of that amount. In addition to a very small population base, another element that prevents a more rapid rate of industrial growth is a complete lack of natural resources, besides oil and gas. The combination of all of those elements discussed above explains most probably the great generosity of the Qatar government in granting the economic assistance to foreign countries in the past.

It can be expected, however, that as the economy of

Part II
Multinational Programs

ministers representing the O.A.U.[2] The African oil-importing countries expressed their concern about the fourfold increase in the price of oil that took place following the October 1973 war, and attempted to obtain some assurances from the Arab countries, guaranteeing them a steady flow of oil supplies and perferential system of oil prices.[3] The exporters of oil were willing to promise a continuing flow of supplies of oil, but at the same time were unwilling to offer a system of preferential prices to the African nations. Following this rather inconclusive meeting in Cairo, numerous further meetings took place between the Arab League and African countries. Starting in the spring of 1974, the Arab countries represented by the Arab League launched a new policy aimed at strengthening the economic and political ties between Arab and African nations. Those ties were designed to create a new political force, the so-called Third World. The Economic Council of the Arab League at its nineteenth session presented a resolution that was subsequently adopted by the Sixth Arab Summit Meeting, calling for a creation of a new framework of economic and financial ties between African and Arab nations. This resolution formed the basis for a formal agreement signed in Cairo on February 18, 1974, providing for the creation of an Arab Bank for Economic Development in Africa.[4] This agreement became effective in September 1974 when it was signed by the required number of member states of the Arab League. The first meeting of the governing council of the bank took place in January 1975 and the board of directors had its first meeting in March 1975. At this meeting, it was decided that the headquarters of the bank would be located in Khartoum (Sudan), and that the bank would start its operations in September 1975.

According to the agreement, the primary objectives of the bank are (1) to participate in the financing of the economic development of African countries, (2) to encourage the participation of Arab capital in development projects in Africa, and (3) to provide the technical assistance for African development.[5] Subsequently, the general provisions stated in the agreement were elaborated in a more detailed way and presented in the "Rules of the Bank."

According to the Rules of the Bank, the highest authority of the bank is placed in the governing council, consisting of one governor and one alternate from each member state.[6] All member countries of the Arab League are also members of the bank. The council, which meets at least once a year, appoints the chairman of the board of directors. The board of directors consists of eleven members, elected for four years. Each country that has subscribed to 200 shares ($20 million) or more has a seat on the board. Those countries included Algeria, Saudi Arabia, the U.A.E., Iraq, Qatar, Kuwait, and Libya. The remaining four members of the board of directors were elected by those countries whose contributions were less than $20 million.[7] The representatives of Syria, Egypt, Morocco, and the P.L.O. were elected to represent those countries. The chairman of the board of directors serves as the chief executive officer of the bank and as president of the bank. Mr. Chedly Ayari, former Tunisian Minister of the National Economy, was appointed as the first president.

The votes of the individual member states represented on the board of governors and board of directors are based on a rather complicated formula that essentially reflects the size of the financial contribution made by each state. According to this formula, Saudi Arabia has 12 percent of the total vote, Libya 10 percent, Iraq 8.5 percent, the U.A.E., Algeria, Qatar, and Kuwait 6.8 percent each, while the remaining member countries have less than 5 percent of the total vote.

The authorized capital of the bank fully subscribed by the members was fixed at $231 million. The largest individual contributions were made by Saudi Arabia ($50 million), Libya ($40 million), Iraq ($30 million), Algeria, Kuwait, Qatar, and the U.A.E. ($20 million each), Morocco ($10 million), Lebanon and Tunisia ($5 million each). Other member countries contributed one million dollars each. Subsequently, however, at a meeting held on November 29, 1975 in Khartoum, the board of directors approved a resolution, presented by the chairman, Mr. Ayari, calling for an increase in the bank's capital from $231 million to $500 million, starting January 1, 1977, and a further increase of an additional $500 million that would raise the subscribed capital to one billion dollars, starting January 1, 1978.[8] In addition to utilizing its own subscribed capital, the bank can also borrow an amount equal to twice the amount of paid-in capital. Thus, the bank, starting in January 1978, has at its disposal financial resources equal to three billion dollars.

Considering the fact that on the average the bank was participating in co-financing various projects in the range of thirty percent of their total cost, it can be concluded that the bank could exercise its impact on approximately ten billion dollars of investment projects in Africa.[9]

The increase in capital from $231 million to one billion dollars was enthusiastically approved by the member countries. There was a unanimous agreement that, considering on the one hand the needs of the African nations, and on the other hand the surpluses of the Arab states, the initial amount of $231 million was totally inadequate and unsatisfactory.

Prior to the official opening of the bank in September 1975, the board of directors held several meetings during the summer months, and announced a set of general rules and principles that would govern the bank's lending policies and operations. Subsequently, most of these rules and principles were published as official Rules of the Bank. Some of the most important rules dealt with the following issues:[10]

1. Loans will be granted only for specific projects that constitute part of a national development plan.
2. Loans will not be granted to cover deficits on the balance of payments.
3. All loans will be based on international bids.
4. The bank reserves the right to supervise the spending of the proceeds of the loan and the implementation of the project.
5. The bank itself will attempt to identify and prepare projects that may be financed by the bank.
6. The bank may lend directly or jointly with other institutions or it may lend to other institutions.
7. Lending will be limited only to African countries that are not members of the Arab League.
8. The amount of each loan should not exceed $10 million.
9. Loans shall carry an interest rate from 1 to 6 percent.
10. The priorities for lending are agriculture, natural resources, and infrastructure and industry.

In addition to the specific regulations concerning its lending policies, the bank also announced two major principles that should constitute the general framework for its operations. The first principle concerned the provision of technical assistance to the borrowing countries, and the second principle dealt with cooperation with other African or international institutions engaged in promoting economic development.

As far as the technical assistance was concerned, the bank anticipated that its role would not be limited to providing financial resources only. On the contrary, it envisaged that one of its main functions would be the offer of professional assistance of many varieties to the developing nations in Africa. Specifically, it was planning to offer its assistance in the preparation of the national development plans, in the preparation of the feasibility studies of specific projects or specific industries, and also in setting up of various educational and professional institutions connected with economic development.[11]

At the same time the board of directors believed that the bank should assume a focal and decisive role in providing the center for cooperation between various agencies concerned with the African economic development. This cooperation would be essentially twofold. In the first place, it would involve co-financing of all projects in which the bank was interested. Secondly, it would involve a formulation of a general framework of cooperation between the bank and the various agencies of the United Nations.[12] Already in May 1975, during the annual assembly of the African Development Bank held in Dakar, Mr. Ayari, president of ABEDA, and Mr. A. Labidi, president of the A.D.B., signed a declaration proclaiming establishment of close cooperation between those two institutions.[13] The declaration emphasized especially the cooperation in sharing information, studies, and research facilities. It also provided for continuous cooperation between the staffs of the two banks, and a formation of joint commissions, if circumstances would warrant it. Finally, the two banks agreed to finance jointly as many projects as their financial resources would allow.

A similar declaration was also signed by Mr. Ayari and Mr. McNamara, president of the International Bank for Reconstruction and Development, at a meeting held in Washington, D.C. on April 17, 1975. On behalf of the I.B.R.D., Mr. McNamara promised to present to Mr. Ayari a list of projects that the two banks could jointly finance. Furthermore, Mr. McNamara offered to make available the technical services and the training facilities of the I.B.R.D. to the professional staff of the ABEDA. Finally, both presidents agreed that their institutions should increase the extent of their cooperation in all areas of their mutual interests.[14]

In addition to signing the declaration of cooperation with the I.B.R.D., Mr. Ayari made similar arrangements with the United Nations Development Program, the United Nations Industrial Development Organization, and the OECD authorities in Paris.

During its formative months of 1975, when the institutional arrangements were being made to create the bank as an operational entity, the bank published a document entitled "A Global Strategy for Arab-African Cooperation."[15] This document eventually became one of the foundation stones of the bank. Basically what this document was attempting to do was to present a five-year plan for the activities of the bank, covering the period between 1975 and 1980.

The document was based on the assumption that the original paid-in capital of $231 million will be eventually increased. According to the plan presented by the bank, starting in 1977 the bank would increase its rate of lending to $250 million annually. If this rate would be maintained for a period of four years, the total amount of money contributed by the bank to African economic development would be in excess of $1.2 billion. If it could be assumed that on the average the bank would contribute to approximately 15 percent of the total cost of each investment project in which it participated, the total impact of the bank's financing would extend to over $10 billion worth of investments over the period 1975–80.

As mentioned earlier, however, shortly after the "Global Strategy" document was published, the member countries decided to increase the subscribed capital to one billion dollars, effective January 1978. This increase had the effect, of course, of modifying the projections expressed in the "Global Strategy."

By the end of 1975, the bank had granted 12 loans, totaling $85 million, for various development projects: $53 million was used to finance seven projects in West Africa,

$22 million was allocated to projects in Zaire and the Democratic Republic of Congo, while only two loans, of $5 million each, were granted to the East African countries of Tanzania and Madagascar.[16] As far as the sectorial distribution of the loans was concerned, 52 percent was allocated for the development of infrastructure, 20 percent for industries, 15 percent for agriculture, and 13 percent for water supply. In the area of infrastructure, most of the loans were used for the construction of railway facilities and highways. All projects in which the bank was involved were also financed by other lenders. The participation of the bank varied from 4 percent to 33 percent of the total cost of a project. The average contribution of the bank amounted to approximately 12 percent of the total cost. This relatively low share of participation could be explained by several factors. First, the bank adopted a definite policy of participating and contributing to as many projects and in as many countries as possible. Second, the bank also followed a policy of limiting the maximum of each loan to $10 million. Those two factors, combined with relatively limited financial resources of the bank, prior to the decision of the board of directors to increase the capital from $231 million to $1 billion, resulted in a relatively low share of participation. All loans were granted for a period of twenty-five years with a rate of interest varying from 2 to 6 percent.[17] It has been calculated that all loans combined had the element of grant equal to about 60 percent.

The first full year of the bank's activities was 1976. During that year the bank granted twenty-one loans totaling $137 million. The average amount of each loan was approximately $7 million. Almost all loans were granted for a period of twenty-five years, and carried a rate of interest of either 2 or 4 percent. Loans were granted to nineteen countries for a variety of purposes. The most frequent object of the loans was, however, classified as rural development. Other purposes of the loans included the construction of highways, electric power stations, hydroelectric installations, and agriculture. Only one loan was granted for industrial investment (a cement factory). During the 1976 fiscal year, the board of directors held several meetings in various parts of Africa. At those meetings, a number of major issues dealing with the financing of African development was discussed. At the meeting held in Addis Ababa on February 28, 1976, the board of directors established formal relations with the Organization of African Unity, and signed an agreement with Mr. W. Eteki M'Boumoua, the executive secretary of the O.A.U., providing for cooperation between the two organizations.[18] The next meeting took place in Kinshasa, Zaire, on May 5, 1976. This meeting was also attended by the presidents or executive secretaries of almost all African agencies dealing with African development.[19] The question of forming a permanent institutional framework for cooperation in financing African development was discussed.

The following June (June 4–6, 1976) a meeting of all Arab financial institutions took place in Riyadh, jointly with the regular meeting of the board of directors. Several important decisions were made at that meeting.[20] Among others, it was decided to set up the Arab Research Center, which would serve as a focal point for economic feasibility studies. It was also agreed to have periodic meetings of representatives of all Arab agencies working in the area of African development. Finally, the board of directors presented a resolution that would extend Arab-African cooperation from the economic and financial fields to cultural and educational relations.

Another meeting of the board of directors of the bank took place in Algiers, October 13–15, 1976. One of the major accomplishments of that meeting was the formation of a permanent Afro-Arab Council of Economic Cooperation.[21] This council was expected to serve as a basic framework and a general focus for all aspects of cooperation between the Arab nations of North Africa and the Middle East, and the Black African countries in the sub-Saharan region.

The last regular meeting of the directors for 1976 was arranged jointly with the second annual meeting of the board of governors of the bank, in November 1976. The most important decision taken at that meeting concerned the increase in the paid-in capital of the bank from $231 million to $500 million, starting January 1, 1977, and an additional increase to one billion dollars, starting January 1, 1978.[22] The official approval of that decision took place at a supplementary meeting, held in December in Cairo, jointly with the Economic Council of the Arab League.[23] Those two meetings actually changed fundamentally the character and scale of the operations of the bank. In the first place, the decisions taken have more than quadrupled the capital of the bank, from less than $250 million to one billion dollars. Secondly, they established another formal link providing for a continuous and permanent cooperation between Africa and Arab nations. Following the resolutions and the recommendations approved in Cairo in December, a special Coordinating Meeting of Arab Development Institutions took place in Khartoum February 13–16, 1977.[24] All national and multinational Arab funds were represented at that meeting, and several proposals were under discussion, aiming at a consolidation of or at least very close collaboration between various Arab financial institutions engaged in economic development. However, no definite arrangement was agreed upon and no definite scheme was set up. The representatives of all funds agreed, however, to continue having regular, annual meetings, at which the problems of financing economic development in African and Arab nations could be examined. The final meeting of

1977 was arranged for Khartoum, on December 3. The most important decision taken by the board of directors at that meeting authorized an increase in the upper limit of the bank's participation in the individual projects. Those limits were increased from 30 percent to 40 percent for large projects, and from 50 to 60 percent for small projects. The aggregate limit however of $10 million on each loan was retained.[25]

Although no complete data are available yet for the whole year of 1977, the preliminary data for the major part of the year strongly indicate that the number and total amount of loans in 1977 were essentially identical with the figures for 1976. In 1977, approximately twenty-five loans were granted, for a total of about $140 million. The length of the loans and the rate of interest charged were also basically the same for 1977 as they were for 1976.

In addition to carrying on its own functions and responsibilities, as provided in the Rules of the Bank, and in addition to using its own financial resources, the bank, from April 1976, became also the administrator of the Special Arab Assistance Fund for Africa (SAAFA). This fund was created in 1974 by the Joint Commission of Oil Ministers of OAPEC (Organization of Arab Oil Exporting Countries) and the Oil Committee of the Organization of African Unity (O.A.U.).[26] The primary function of SAAFA was to provide interest-free loans to African countries importing oil that were experiencing balance of payments difficulties as a result of the fourfold increase in the price of oil in late 1973 and early 1974. SAAFA was created at the request of the African countries, represented by the O.A.U., and until the end of 1975 was administered by the offices of the Arab League in Cairo. As the staff of the Arab League was, however, not too well equipped to manage this kind of financial operations, the O.A.U. requested that the management of the SAAFA be placed in the hands of the

African Development Bank in Abidjan (Ivory Coast). The Arab countries preferred, however, to keep the management of the SAAFA in Arab hands, and decided therefore to transfer it to ABEDA in Khartoum. Between February 1974 and December 1975, SAAFA provided $171 million in loans to thirty-three African oil-importing countries. The loans were granted interest-free, for a period of twenty-five years with ten years' grace period. Considering the conditions under which the loans were given, they could be looked upon more as grants than commercial loans.

Between May and December 1976, the bank, using the SAAFA funds, granted three loans for a total of $56 million. In February 1977, the OAPEC countries decided to continue the SAAFA program for an indefinite period of time, and agreed to allocate a sum of $360 million for further emergency loans to African countries, with ABEDA acting as administrator of the funds.

Although the bank has been in operation for a relatively short period of time, and its activities cover only two full years (1976–77), several conclusions can be presented.

The bank constitutes the first, and so far the only, formal and official link between the members of the Arab League and sub-Saharan African countries, designed to foster economic cooperation between those two groups of nations.[27] It has been stated on numerous occasions by the African press and African statesmen that the primary function of the bank is to channel part of the surplus of petro-dollars accumulated by Arab oil-exporting countries to the developing oil-importing nations of Africa. Although the initial discussions concerning the formation of the bank took place at the request of the O.A.U. in December 1973 and January 1974, following the quadrupling of the prices of oil, the member countries of the bank as well as the executives of the bank very strongly deny that there exist any links between the new prices of oil, the surpluses of petro-dollars, and the decision to provide aid to the developing nations of Africa. They maintain that there is absolutely no connection between the activities of the bank and the problem of recycling part of the petro-dollars back to the African oil importers.

Mr. Ayari, the president of the bank, discussed this topic on several occasions, and although admitting that the high prices paid for oil have caused many financial difficulties in African countries, he stated very emphatically that there should be "an African solution for the African oil problem."[28] According to Mr. Ayari, the statistical data clearly indicate that sub-Saharan Africa produces over 130 million tons of oil per year (primarily Nigeria [100 million], Gabon, and Congo) while it consumes only about 15 million tons per annum. Thus, he believed that the sub-Saharan oil exporters, primarily Nigeria, should be responsible for finding a solution to the financial difficulties stemming from higher prices of oil paid by the sub-Saharan oil importers.[29]

Although the figures quoted by Mr. Ayari are undoubtedly correct, nonetheless they do not change the fact that the increase in the price of oil has caused much greater financial difficulties on the balance of payments of African countries than it did to the European importers of oil. According to the 1977 Middle East Survey, the relative impact has been much heavier, and most likely will continue to be so, on the poor African countries than on the relatively rich European nations.[30] Such a situation is generally caused by two factors: first, the imports of oil constitute a much larger share of total imports in most African countries than they do in the European countries, and secondly, the European countries have the opportunity to increase their export to the Arab countries as part of the recycling process of the petro-dollars, while the African nations, in most cases, have very little to offer to the Arab surplus nations.[31]

The idea of establishing the bank undoubtedly had, and will continue to have, a positive impact on forging closer economic and political links between Arab and African nations. It also represents a definite manifestation of the generosity of the Arab oil exporters toward their less fortunate neighbors in Africa.

The crucial question remains, however, as to what will be the tangible impact of the flow of funds via the bank on the general economic development of Africa. There are many indications that such an impact will not be very decisive, simply because the magnitude of the financial flows generated by the bank is rather limited.

According to the statements made by the I.B.R.D. in Washington, D.C., in 1974, for example, Africa received about $1.2 billion of aid from all sources; the flows provided by the bank accounted for slightly more than 10 percent of that amount.[32] Furthermore, as the statistical data of the bank indicate, the average size of a loan from the bank is about $7 million, and most countries have received only one loan so far.

Finally, it should be emphasized that the bank has not been utilizing its available resources as much and as fast as it maybe should. In 1977, for example, the total financial resources of the bank totaled $3 billion ($1 billion being the subscribed capital plus $2 billion that the bank could borrow). Nonetheless, the bank granted less than $159 million in loans. It utilized, therefore, less than 5 percent of its available resources. During the twenty-seven months of its operations, between September 1975 and December 1977, it distributed less than $400 million in loans, i.e., slightly more than 10 percent of its resources.

In spite of the numerous statements and proclamations made in 1976 that the flow of aid would substantially increase in 1977, the actual flow in 1977 remained essentially the same as in the previous year.[33] There are several factors that could possibly account for this rather low and slow rate of lending. The bank is apparently confronted by a relative shortage of professional manpower on its staff that could evaluate, appraise, and process applications for loans.[34] At the same time, the African borrowers are faced with the same shortage of manpower in preparing development plans and feasibility studies, and in presenting applications for loans. It appears that both sides have to rely to a large extent on the services provided by the foreign experts, usually sent to Africa by the French or British governments as part of their foreign aid programs.[35]

It is also very likely that sub-Saharan Africa in its present stage of development may simply lack effective opportunities for productive investments. According to a recent comprehensive study of lending abroad by the American banks conducted by the Federal Reserve Board, it appears that American banks had $164 billion of outstanding foreign loans as of June 30, 1977.[36] Of this amount only $1.9 billion was given to African nations, and that included not only the sub-Saharan states but also Arab countries in North Africa. It may be also interesting to compare the $1.9 billion lent to Africa with $6 billion of loans granted to the OPEC nations.

The limited impact that the bank has most likely had so far on the development process of Black Africa should not be construed as criticism of the bank per se. Even if its impact is somewhat limited, nonetheless the bank represents an economic and political link between Arab and African nations, and it also represents one of the channels for the flow of capital that may make a contribution to the economic progress of the African continent. It appears also very likely that, in the long run, the most important impact of the bank might not be limited to the financial aid that it provides, but it might be rather centered on its function as a focal point of cooperation among the European technology, Arab money, and African natural resources.[37] It is also likely that the impact will not be limited to the economic effects but may also extend to the cultural, social, and political aspects. It may represent a basis for the unity of the Third World, confronting the affluent, industrialized nations of Europe and North America.

A final evaluation of the bank would be incomplete without recalling again the fact that the bank acted also, from April 1976, as an administrator of SAAFA.[38] Although officially SAAFA exists as a totally independent entity, and separate from the bank, nevertheless the practical connection between those two institutions is very close indeed. The most relevant link between them is based on the fact that most of their financial resources originate from the same group of countries, namely, the leading Arab oil exporters. They have provided funds for SAAFA and they also provide the bulk of funds for the bank. Therefore, in addition to approximately $400 million provided by the Arab oil exporters to the bank, one should also add an additional approximately $225 million dollars provided by the same Arab oil exporters to SAAFA.[39] Thus, the total financial assistance of the Arab oil exporters to sub-Saharan African countries over the three-year period of 1974-77 through the Bank would exceed $600 million. Even if it is assumed that there may be a certain degree of validity in the criticism that the total amount of financing provided by the member countries of the bank may be somewhat limited, nevertheless, when it is considered that essentially the same group of lenders to the bank acted also as a group of donors to SAAFA, then most probably most of the economic experts would agree that the total impact made by the flow of money from the Arab surplus countries to the developing nations in the sub-Saharan region is rather substantial and may have significant effect on the progress of their development process. In the short run, obviously the effects of SAAFA financing are important, while in the long run, most likely the loans provided by the bank will exert their impact.

Notes

1. UNCTAD, *Economic Co-operation among Developing Countries* (TD/B/AC.19/1), December 1975, pp. 23–25.
2. ABEDA, *Selected Press Clippings,* February 1976, p. 68.
3. ABEDA, *Annual Report 1975,* pp. 21–24.
4. UNCTAD, *Financial Co-operation among Developing Countries* (TD/B/AC.19/R.8/Add. 1), October 1975, p. 80.
5. UNCTAD, *Economic Co-operation and Integration among Developing Countries* (TD/B/609/Add.1.Vol.IV), August 1976, pp. 54 ff.
6. ABEDA, *Principles Governing the Bank's Policy on the Financing of Development Projects;* ABEDA, *Financial Regulations;* ABEDA, *Accord Général Portant Création de la Banque (BADEA).*
7. UNCTAD, *Economic Co-operation and Integration among Developing Countries.* (TD/B/609/Vol. II), May 1976, p. 97.
8. ABEDA, *Annual Report 1975,* p. 29.
9. Ibid., pp. 18–19.
10. ABEDA, *Rules Governing the Financial Operations of the Bank.*
11. UNCTAD, *Economic Co-operation and Integration among Developing Countries* (TD/B/609/Add.1/Vol.V), August 1976, pp. 56–58.
12. UNCTAD (TD/B/AC.19/R.8/Add.1), p. 82.
13. ABEDA, *Annual Report 1975,* p. 61.
14. Ibid., p. 62.
15. Ibid., p. 26.
16. Ibid., p. 12.
17. Ibid., p. 20.
18. ABEDA, *Press Release* no. 5/76, 1 March 1976.
19. ABEDA, *Press Release* no. 10/76, 5 May 1976.
20. ABEDA, *Press Release* No. 14/76, 6–7 June 1976.
21. ABEDA, *Press Release* no. 31/76, 21 October 1976.
22. ABEDA, *Press Release* no. 32/76, 23 October 1976.
23. ABEDA, *Press Release* no. 33/76, 3 November 1976.
24. ABEDA, *Press Release* no. 1/77, 13 February 1977.
25. ABEDA, *Press Release* no. 18/77, 3 December 1977.
26. UNCTAD (TD/AC.19/R.8/Add.1), pp. 72–75; and *International Financial Co-operation for Development* (TD/188/Supp.1/Add.1), February 1976.
27. ABEDA, *Annual Report 1975,* pp. 21–24.
28. ABEDA, *Collection of Speeches by Dr. Chedly Ayari,* November 1976, p. 16.

29. Ibid.

30. *The Middle East Yearbook 1977*, p. 60.

31. UNCTAD, *Trade Prospects and Capital Needs of Developing Countries* (TD/B/C.3/134 and Add.1), April 1976.

32. ABEDA, *Collection of Speeches by Dr. Chedly Ayari*, November, 1976, p. 10.

33. ABEDA, *Press Release* nos. 15/77, 16/77, 17/77, 23 October 1977, 27 October 1977, 15 November 1977.

34. *The Middle East Yearbook 1977*, p. 62.

35. Yoon S. Park, *Oil Money and the World Economy* (Boulder, Colo.: Westview Press, 1976), pp. 142 ff.

36. "Data Given on U.S. Bank Lending Abroad," *International Herald Tribune*, 8 February 1978.

37. ABEDA, *Selected Press Clippings*, February 1976, p. 5.

38. ABEDA, *Press Release* no. 17/76 and 18/76, 27 June 1976.

39. ABEDA, *Collection of Speeches by Dr. Chedly Ayari*, November 1976, pp. 41–42.

6
Arab Fund for Economic and Social Development (AFESD)

A plan to form a fund for economic and social development of the Arab countries had been under discussion by the members of the Arab League since the early 1950s. However, a specific proposal was made only in August of 1967, when the government of Kuwait formally recommended at the conference of the Arab finance ministers held in Baghdad that the Arab Fund for Economic and Social Development be established. The following May, the Council for Arab Economic Unity of the Arab League gave its official approval for the formation of the fund, and the government of Kuwait, as the sponsor of the fund, pledged KD 30 million toward the authorized capital of KD 100 million.[1] On May 16, 1968, seventeen members of the Arab League signed the agreement to form AFESD. In spite of the Kuwaiti contribution, AFESD remained inactive until December 1970, when other Arab governments pledged their contributions to the fund, which raised the paid-in subscriptions to over KD 80 million (equal to about $280 million).[2]

The major contributions to the fund were made by Libya (KD 12 million), Egypt (KD 10.5 million), Iraq (KD 7.5 million), Abu Dhabi (KD 6 million), and Algeria (KD 4 million). Smaller amounts of money were contributed by the remaining members of the Arab League, except Saudi

Arabia. It was believed that the reluctance of the Saudi government to join the fund was based on two issues: In the first place the Saudi government at that time preferred to concentrate on direct bilateral loans and grants, and secondly, as far as multilateral channels were concerned, the Saudi government was focusing its attention on its own plan for the Islamic Development Bank.[3] Finally, however, at the end of 1974, Saudi Arabia decided to join the fund, and the total subscribed capital was increased to KD 100 million (approximately $350 million). Kuwait, however, has remained the largest single subscriber to the fund. Its subscription amounted to 30 percent of all shares outstanding, while the Saudi contribution amounted to 20 percent.

According to the charter of AFESD, signed by seventeen members of the Arab League in Cairo on May 16, 1968, the purpose of the fund is twofold: first, to finance various projects in the Arab states aiming at economic and social development, and second, to encourage investment of private and public capital in those projects.[4]

A very definite priority should be given to projects "vital to Arab unity and to joint Arab projects" (article 2). The membership in the fund is open to all members of the Arab League, and the capital of the fund is equal to KD 100 million. Subsequently, in 1975, the capital was increased to KD 400 million (approximately $1.4 billion). The subscribed capital was divided into 10,000 shares. Kuwait subscribed to 3,000 shares and Saudi Arabia to 2,000. Article 7 of the charter provided that 10 percent of the subscribed capital should be paid in immediately, while the balance would be paid in ten equal installments over a period of ten years. The resources of the fund would consist of its subscribed capital and the reserves. In addition, the fund was authorized to borrow on international capital markets, through bonds or otherwise, an additional amount equal to twice the paid-in capital.

Articles 13–17 of the charter described in a rather detailed way the methods of operations of the fund. Essentially, the function of the fund was limited to lending its resources or guaranteeing loans. The fund should not participate in the management of any project and it should not engage in or interfere with the political affairs of any country.

The governing bodies of the fund consisted of the board of governors, board of directors, and a director-general, chairman of the board of directors.[5] The board of governors consists of a representative of each member country, elected for a period of five years. The board should meet at least once a year, and the voting is based on the number of shares held by each member. Saudi Arabia and Kuwait had, therefore, 50 percent of the votes on the board. The board of directors, elected by the board of governors, consisted of four full-time economic experts who actually performed the managerial function for the fund. The board of directors had the duty to appoint the director-general of the fund, who also acted as the chairman of the board of directors. In effect, he was the chief executive officer of the fund.[6]

The charter provided that the Minister of Finance of Kuwait shall act as trustee and depository agent of the fund. The offices of the fund would be located in Kuwait. Mr. Saeb Jaroudi, Lebanese Minister of National Economy, was appointed as the first director-general of the fund, and Mr. Abdlatif Al-Hamad, director-general of the Kuwait Fund, was appointed as one of the directors. Although the charter establishing the fund had been signed in 1968 and the subscriptions paid in in 1970 (except by Saudi Arabia), the fund remained totally inactive until 1973. During that year it granted three loans, to Tunisia, Syria, and the Democratic Republic of Yemen, totaling KD 7.2 million.[7] The projects for which the funds were provided included an electric power station, a fish-processing plant, and oil storage tanks. All loans were granted for a period of twenty years with five years' grace period, and carried an interest rate of between 4 to 6 percent.

In addition to granting loans, the fund concentrated in the initial stage of its operation on establishing close working relations with the Council of Arab Economic Unity, the Abu Dhabi Fund, the Kuwait Fund, and various agencies of the United Nations. The fund also made several studies dealing with closer monetary and financial cooperation among the Arab states. A major study presented by the fund discussed the formation of an Arab Monetary Union.[8]

The fund firmly believed that such a union would be a decisive and indispensable step toward closer economic relations between the members of the Arab League. During 1974, the first complete year of the fund's activities, the fund granted five loans totaling KD 29.9 million.[9] As in the previous year, the loans were granted for twenty years, with five or six years of grace, and with an interest of 4 or 6 percent. The loans were granted to Egypt (fertilizer plant), Algeria (port facilities), Sudan (highway), Yemen Arab Republic (power stations), and Syria (meat and dairy products). The loans provided by the fund accounted, on the average, for 20 percent of the total cost of each project. In addition to granting loans for specific projects, most of the effort of the fund was directed toward more general activities aimed at the formation of a framework that would facilitate closer economic relations among the Arab states. The fund, for example, continued its study of the Arab Monetary Union, and initiated two new studies. One of the studies focused on the pan-Arab highway system while the other analyzed a pan-Arab telecommunication network. The fund also undertook some preliminary steps toward the creation of a large-scale agricultural research facility in Sudan. It was expected that eventually this facility would develop into a several-million-acre research farm that would provide a start for a massive program aimed at improvement in agriculture in all Arab countries. Several plans were presented at that time, indicating that the Arab League and the fund were looking at Sudan as the agricultural center for the whole Arab world.[10] During 1974, a special task was placed in the hands of the fund. The Organization of the Arab Oil Exporting Countries requested the fund to administer a special account of OAPEC. This account, consisting of $80 million, was designed to provide emergency loans to developing countries that were experiencing balance of payments difficulties created by the increased price of oil. The total amount of $80 million was distributed in interest-free loans for twenty years, with ten years of grace.[11] In effect, those loans had more a character of a grant than a regular loan.

The fund created also in 1974 a special agency called Investment Servicing and Promotion Unit. The primary function of that unit was to mobilize funds from various Arab sources and channel them toward specific investment projects sponsored by the Fund. Those funds would be used, in effect, in co-financing the projects jointly with the fund. During the fiscal year of 1974, four additional countries (Saudi Arabia, Oman, Somalia, and Mauritania) joined the fund, increasing the total membership to twenty. At the same time, as the financial situation of the oil-exporting countries improved substantially, following increase in oil prices, the fund decided to shorten by 50 percent the remaining period for subscription of the capital by the member countries.[12] The fiscal year of 1975 witnessed further expansion of the activities of the fund. It granted ten new loans for a total of KD 56 million.[13] Almost 50 percent of that amount was granted in three loans to Egypt for an improvement in the Cairo water and sewage system, and for a cement factory. Loans were granted to Sudan, Morocco, and Algeria for modernization of their telecommunication systems. Further loans were made to Jordan (highway)

Tunisia (gas treatment), Sudan (highways), Democratic Republic of Yemen (port facilities), and Yemen Arab Republic (water supply). All loans were granted for twenty years and carried an interest payment of 4 or 6 percent, with the usual grace period of four or five years.

During the fiscal year 1975, the fund pursued further its interest in the massive agricultural research facilities in Sudan.[14] In August, a formal agreement was signed between the fund and the Sudanese government providing for a formation of a ten-year plan aimed at doubling the agricultural output of Sudan. In September, a treaty was also signed with the Abu Dhabi Fund and the Kuwait Fund.

The primary objective of that treaty was to create a framework for regular consultations and increased cooperation between various funds providing economic assistance for development in Arab countries. A similar agreement was also signed between the fund and the United Nations Development Program. Another agreement was signed with the United Nations Economic Commission for Western Asia (headquartered in Beirut, Lebanon), providing for a series of grants from the fund to the commission. Those grants would be used to finance studies analyzing various aspects of closer economic relations among the Arab nations.

It is apparent that in 1975, the fund became gradually aware that in spite of its objectives stated in its charter and defining its functions as a source of financing various projects aimed at Arab economic unity, it has been rather difficult to find such projects.[15] All loans except one, granted during the three year period 1973–75, were for specific projects located in one country and had no bearing at all on fostering Arab economic unity. Only one loan, for improvements in the telecommunication system, involved two countries, i.e., Morocco and Algeria.

At the fourth annual meeting of the board of governors,

held in Kuwait on April 15, 1975, it was decided to increase the capital of the fund to KD 400 million (approximately $1.4 billion), and to admit Palestine as the twenty-first member of the fund.[16] This decision of the board indicated very clearly that the member countries envisaged an increasingly important role of the fund in promoting the economic and social development of those Arab countries which were not fortunate to be exporters of oil and to have huge surpluses of petro-dollars. By increasing the capital of the fund to almost $1.5 billion, the board also increased the borrowing capacity of the fund to almost $3 billion. By doing so, the board of governors placed the fund in a leading position as one of the most significant sources of investment capital for the development of the relatively less affluent Arab countries.

On the basis of the operations of the fund over a period of three years, several general conclusions could be drawn. Some of the conclusions are definitely on the positive side, while others seem to indicate certain gaps and deficiencies in the functioning of the fund.

In addition to providing its own funds, AFESD tried to act as an agent for channeling private Arab capital for various projects, either by organizing groups of banks or private investors who would provide financial resources, or by selling its own bonds. According to its charter, the fund was authorized to sell bonds equal to double the amount of its capital. Another positive accomplishment of the fund was in its emphasis on financing projects in the area of public utilities.

This was a new and somewhat controversial idea. In the past, most of the lending by the majority of the various funds in the Middle East, as much as in other parts of the world, was concentrated largely on financing industrial or agricultural projects that could directly show their profitability. AFESD believed, however, that development of public utilities presented a direct contribution to the economic development of the whole country.[17] From its very beginning AFESD cooperated very closely with the Kuwait Fund in undertaking joint feasibility studies, in offering loans on the basis of the feasibility studies prepared by the Kuwait Fund, in jointly sponsoring specific projects, and in exchanging information about its activities and plans in general.[18] Subsequently, when the Abu Dhabi Fund for Arab Economic Development was formed, the Arab Fund, jointly with the Kuwait Fund, established a very close working relationship. It should be emphasized that such a joint cooperative effort among various national funds in the Middle East is definitely an exception rather than a rule. Although from an economic point of view such a cooperation would be most beneficial and highly productive, nevertheless other factors, usually of political nature, have prevented such a cooperative effort from taking place.

Although the charter of the fund and numerous statements included in its annual reports emphasize very strongly that the fund should concentrate its effort on financing multinational projects that would contribute to economic unity and economic integration among Arab states, actual experience clearly indicates that the fund has engaged mostly in "conventional style, country-project lending"[19] that would contribute very little, if anything, to Arab economic unity. The main reason for such a divergence between the policy proclamations and the reality of life is most likely the fact that it is much easier to find relatively small, country projects rather than big, regional-integration schemes. An examination of the operations of the Arab Fund indicates that the fund has operated in essentially the same way as the other funds did in Kuwait, Saudi Arabia, or Abu Dhabi. In a way, then, instead of being a truly all-comprehensive *Arab* fund, the Arab Fund acted simply as another national fund. According to Prof. Solimar Demir, "In order for the Arab Fund to serve Arab economic integration, a re-evaluation of its operational policies needs to be undertaken immediately in order to gear its future operations toward the broad policy goals that the Arab Fund was established to fulfill."[20]

Frequently, a comparison has been made between the Arab Fund and the Kuwait Fund, and whenever the organizational structures and the method of operations were compared, very significant differences could be detected.[21] The Kuwait Fund from its very beginning has been characterized by the informality of its operations and simplicity of its structure. The Arab Fund, on the other hand, seems to have a very elaborate and complicated structure and its operations are rather very formal, slow, and involved. Most likely, one of the problems that prevented a smooth operation of the Arab Fund was the difficulty in recruiting professional staff that would be truly representative of the international composition of its membership. Not being able to recruit economic and financial experts from the Arab countries, the Arab Fund had to rely frequently on assistance from experts provided by the I.M.F., the International Bank, or the OECD. It seems likely that a shortage of permanent professional staff well acquainted with the region imposed certain handicaps on the operations of the Arab Fund.[22]

Occasionally a criticism has been voiced that the Arab Fund has not been utilizing its full capacity and its full opportunities, as far as lending is concerned. It appears that such a criticism is well founded. The aggregate lending capacity of the Arab Fund is truly enormous: it consists of $1.4 billion of its own funds contributed by the member countries, plus $2.8 billion that it can borrow on the international financial markets. In total, therefore, the Arab Fund has an aggregate lending capacity of $4.2 billion. So far, however, during its three years of operations, 1973–75, it has lent only approximately \$325 million. It means, therefore, that over 90 percent of the lending potential has not yet been utilized; so far the fund has been operating at less than 10 percent of its capacity.

Finally, there are many indications that the Arab Fund is under a rather strong influence from Kuwait.[23]

The government of Kuwait promoted the idea of the Arab Fund during the early 1960s, it organized it, and it also provided one-third of its capital. Furthermore, Mr. Al-Hamad, the executive director of the Kuwait Fund since the start of its operations, has been appointed as one of the directors of the Arab Fund.

Finally, the head office of the fund is located in Kuwait. A certain degree of similarity could be detected in the relationship between Kuwait and the Arab Fund, and on the other hand, between Saudi Arabia and the Islamic Development Bank.[24] The very close ties that seem to exist between the Kuwait government and the Arab Fund find an almost identical reflection in the close ties existing between the Saudi government and the Islamic Development Bank, located in Jeddah. As far as the operations of the fund in the past are concerned, it seems very likely that there may exist a close connection between the lack of utilization of its full lending capacity, and the fund's concentration on relatively small projects, limited to one individual country. According to its charter, the Arab Fund should engage in large schemes that would promote Arab economic unity and integration. It is possible that as certain political difficulties combined with a shortage of professional staff have prevented the fund from sponsoring and financing those large multinational integration schemes, the fund has decided to operate for the time being in relatively low gear and to limit its activities to somewhat minor industrial or agricultural investments. At the same time, the fund has been pursuing two major projects that may have an impact on the Arab community of nations in the future. One study dealt with the Arab Monetary Union, and the other focused on the agricultural development in Sudan. It was anticipated that the plan aiming at a substantial increase of agricultural output in Sudan would have an impact on the supply of food for a large number of countries in the Middle East. It is very likely that once this plan is implemented it will make a contribution to closer economic ties among the Arab countries. However, the chances for the implementation of the plan for the Arab Monetary Union appear at the moment extremely small. It seems that the diversity of economic and financial conditions in various Arab countries is simply too great, and the political differences too substantial, to offer a fair chance of success for a monetary union of the Arab nations in the foreseeable future.

The largest project sponsored and financed by the AFESD that is encountering some difficulties at the moment is the Arab Authority for Agricultural Investment and Development in Sudan, frequently called the "triple A-I-D." Its main function is to implement a huge, comprehensive, and integrated plan aimed at the development of agriculture in Sudan.[25] The project was discussed for over three years, and finally was approved by the fund. A special administrative machinery was set up in order to implement this plan. An independent agency, the triple A-I-D has been formed and placed in full control of the scheme; its initial budget has been fixed at KD 750 million (approximately $2.1 billion). The triple A-I-D shall be totally independent of the Sudanese government, as well as from the regular administrators of the fund.

The fund originally envisaged that the work of implementation of the agricultural project would start in 1976. Numerous delays, however, postponed the start of its operations. According to the first stage plan, prepared by the fund, and approved by the Sudanese government, it was expected that $6.6 billion would be spent during the 1976–80 period. It was also anticipated that by the end of this period, Sudan would provide 42 percent of the Arab world's imports of vegetable oils, 20 percent of its sugar, more than 50 percent of its animal fodder, and about 25 percent of its wheat. But those production targets are looking increasingly unrealistic because of the slow rate of implementation of the existing projects, because of inflation, delays in getting new projects off the ground, and most importantly, because of the setbacks that took place in the process of establishing the authority of the whole project.

According to the most recent information, there remains one major obstacle that prevents the Authority from starting its functioning.[26]

This obstacle consists of a disagreement between the member states of the fund concerning the appointment of the president of the authority, who would act as its chief executive officer. The fund has proposed Dr. Khalid Ali, an Iraqi national, the author of the original plan, and staff member of the fund, as the president. Apparently, the government of Egypt has decided to veto his appointment, and suggested instead Mr. Sayed Marei, an Egyptian national, and a former minister of agriculture in Egypt. In late 1977 and in the early part of 1978, several meetings took place between the representatives of the fund and the Egyptian government, but no agreement could be reached concerning the appointment of the president of the authority. In the meantime, the huge plan for the development of agriculture in Sudan remains dormant.

Notes

1. Robert Stephens, *The Arabs' New Frontier* (London: Temple Smith Ltd., 1973).

2. UNCTAD, *Economic Co-operation and Integration among Developing Countries* (TD/B/609/vol.11), May 1976, pp. 98–100.

3. Michael Field, *A Hundred Million Dollars a Day* (London: Sidgwick & Jackson, 1975), p. 153.

4. AFESD, *Agreement Establishing the Arab Fund for Economic and Social Development* (Kuwait, 1968).

5. Ibid., p. 21.

6. UNCTAD, *Economic Co-operation and Integration among Developing Countries* (TD/B/609/Add.1/vol. V), August 1976, pp. 73, 87.

7. AFESD, *Annual Report 1973*.

8. Ibid.

9. AFESD, *Annual Report 1974*.

10. Ibid.

11. Ibid.

12. Ibid.

13. AFESD, *Annual Report 1975*.

14. Ibid.

15. Ibid.

16. Ibid.

17. UNCTAD, *Financial Co-operation among Developing Countries* (TD/B/AC.19/R.8/Add.1), October 1975, pp. 69–70.

18. Michael Field, *A Hundred Million Dollars a Day*, pp. 153 ff.

19. Solimar Demir, *The Kuwait Fund and the Political Economy of Arab Regional Development* (New York: Praeger, 1976), p. 95.

20. Ibid., p. 97.

21. Ibid., p. 87.

22. Ibid., p. 92.

23. Robert Stephens, *The Arabs' New Frontier*, pp. 68–69.

24. Solimar Demir, *The Arabs' New Frontier*, pp. 68–69.

25. "Arab Rivalries Delay Big Sudan Project," *Saudi Gazette*, 12 February 1978.

26. Ibid.

7
Islamic Development Bank (I.D.B.)

A proposal to create the Islamic Development Bank was first presented at the Islamic Conference of Finance Ministers held in Jeddah, on December 18, 1973.[1] A formal declaration of intent was approved by the conference, and a preparatory committee was appointed. The committee consisted of three members, and included a former prime minister of Malaysia, the governor of the Saudi Arabian Monetary Agency (SAMA), and the governor of the State Bank of Pakistan. The committee prepared a set of articles of agreement that were presented to and approved by a subsequent conference of finance ministers of the Islamic states held in August 1974. The first meeting of the governors took place in Riyadh under the chairmanship of the Minister of State for National Economy for Saudi Arabia. At that meeting the governors elected Dr. Ahmad Mohamad Ali, former Deputy Minister of Education for Saudi Arabia, as president and chairman of the board of executive directors. The bank officially started its activities on October 20, 1975.[2]

The articles of agreement approved in August 1974 define and describe the purposes, functions, and structure of the Bank.[3] According to the articles, the purpose of the bank is to promote economic development and social progress of the member countries and in Moslem communities in nonmember countries.

According to article 2, the bank is to participate in equity

122

capital of various investment projects, to invest in economic and social infrastructure projects, to make loans to private and public enterprises, to borrow capital on international capital markets, to engage in activities promoting foreign trade, to provide technical assistance, to undertake research in economic and social areas, and finally, to cooperate with other institutions of similar character.

Article 3 provides that the membership is open to all country members of the Islamic Conference. On August 12, 1974, twenty-seven countries joined. The initial membership of the bank included almost all Arab countries plus Guinea, Indonesia, Malaysia, Mali, Pakistan, Senagal, Bangladesh, and Turkey. During the subsequent year three additional countries joined the bank: Syria, Afghanistan, and Lebanon. By the end of 1976, however, the membership formalities were not yet completed by Mali and Senegal, and it remained doubtful if those two countries would actually become active members of the bank.

Article 4 stated that the unit of account of the bank shall be known as Islamic Dinar, equal to one Special Drawing Right (SDR) of the International Monetary Fund. The authorized stock of the bank was equal to 2 billion Islamic Dinars, divided into 200,000 shares. The initial subscribed capital of the bank was declared to be equal to 750 million Islamic Dinars. The largest subscribers to the capital of the bank were Saudi Arabia (200 million I.D.), Libya (125 million I.D.), and United Arab Emirates and Kuwait (100 million I.D. each). The initial subscription of other member countries varied from 25 to 2.5 million I.D. The Saudi Arabian Monetary Agency was appointed as the trustee and depository of the bank. The temporary headquarters of the bank were located in the former royal Niaba Palace in Jeddah, while the permanent headquarters building was being constructed in Jeddah.

Articles 12–21 described in a rather detailed way the

operations, lending policies, and management structure of the bank. The articles very strongly emphasize the fact that the lending policies should be always based on very strict financial considerations and prudent banking principles. At the same time, however, whenever special circumstances warrant it, the general economic and social situation of the prospective borrower should also be considered. In granting equity capital, the bank should not attempt to acquire a controlling interest in the enterprise concerned, nor should it attempt to assume managerial functions. Although the articles do not mention anything about charging interest, they stress that a service charge equal to between 4 and 6 percent of the loan should be charged.

The operations of the bank were divided into two completely separate categories. The first type of operations, called the Ordinary Operations, should be financed by the ordinary capital subscribed by the members. Obviously, this type of operation would constitute the bulk of the bank's activities. The second type of activities was called Special Operations and should be financed by a special fund. The Special Operations consisted essentially of grants given to Moslem communities in nonmembers countries. The resources of the special fund would originate from revenues resulting from the regular transactions conducted within the framework of Ordinary Operations.

According to article 28, the governing bodies of the bank would consist of the board of governors and the board of executive directors, in addition to the president of the bank and one or more vice-presidents. Each member country was authorized to appoint one governor. According to the articles of agreement all powers of the bank are vested in the board of governors. At the same time, however, the board of governors is authorized to delegate most of its powers to the board of executive directors, which is responsible for the actual operation and management of the bank. The board of executive directors shall consist of ten financial and economic experts, appointed for a period of three years by the board of governors. A special formula was decided upon to determine the appointment procedures. Each of the largest shareholders of the bank (Saudi Arabia, Libya, Kuwait, and the U.A.E.) were authorized to appoint one director each, while the remaining member countries of the bank could elect the remaining six executive directors. Subsequently, six financial experts from Egypt, Niger, Guinea, Pakistan, Malaysia, and Algeria were appointed as directors. The president of the bank, who is also a chairman of the board of executive directors, is to be elected by the governors for a period of five years. The president is the chief executive officer of the bank.[4]

The member countries had also decided that the bank should be considered as an international entity, subject to all sorts of immunities, freedoms, and exemptions from national laws and regulations. Specifically, the bank should enjoy an immunity of its assets and noninterference with its proceedings, and freedom from all national taxes. At the same time, however, the bank was enjoined from participation in any political activity. The voting power within the board of governors was based on the number of shares held by each member country. It was determined, therefore, that Saudi Arabia should have 23 percent of vote, Libya 15 percent, United Arab Emirates 13 percent, and Kuwait 12 percent, while the voting power of all other member countries varied from 3.5 to 0.85 percent.

In December 1976, the bank published its first annual report, covering the period of fifteen months from October 1975 to December 1976.[5] The report presented a detailed picture of the activities of the bank during that period, and at the same time it also expressed several statements of policies concerning various activities of the bank. Essentially, those statements of policies presented an elaboration of the general principles stated in the articles of agreement. The report strongly emphasized that the bank would "operate on the basis of sound economic principles . . . paying due regard to safeguarding its interests in respect of its financing."[6]

Another very important principle announced in the report expressed the bank's determination to concentrate on joint-venture projects that would include the participation of other national or international financial institutions, and also to concentrate on projects that contribute to economic cooperation and integration among the Moslem nations. The report also stressed again the fact that the bank would be determined to follow sound banking principles in its lending policies, and attempt to exercise its full authority in providing for the safety and security of its investments. Although on special occasions the bank might engage in program lending, the bulk of its operations should be focused on project lending.

During the first year of its operation, the board of executive directors, in addition to recruiting the staff and providing the basis for a start of its activities, attempted to formulate the guidelines for its lending policies. At the meetings held in the early part of 1976, the board stated several basic guidelines for its subsequent operations. It decided that all of its lending should be in the form of joint financing, with other international institutions. It decided also that its staff should consist of highly professional experts with a high degree of competence and expertise. Finally, it decided that in all cases it should follow "the Islamic principles of Shariah."[7] One of its very first ventures was the formation of the Technical Projects Research Center. The center was established jointly with the Saudi Development Fund, the Kuwait Development Fund, the Abu Dhabi Development Fund, and the Arab Bank for Economic Development in Africa. Its primary function was to provide facility for the identification, evaluation, and appraisal of potential projects suitable for the lending operations of the bank. At the same time, the center would serve as a training base for the staff of the bank. The board of directors approved also the operating budget (salaries, office expenses, etc.) for 1975–76 and for the subsequent year of 1977. The budget for the first year was equal to 7.5 million Dinars while for the second year it amounted to 9.5 million I.D. The board of directors approved also the overall lending policies of the bank during its first year of operation. By the end of 1976 the bank had invested more than 300 million I.D. and received 18 million I.D. as profit on its investments. This sum of 18 million I.D. was placed in a special account that would be used in the subsequent years as a source of funds for Special Operations, i.e., providing grants to Moslem communities in non-Moslem countries.[8]

There are several features that characterize the operations of the bank during the first year of its existence. It appears that the bank experienced a very promising start. In spite of the fact that it became operational only in October 1975, and in spite of the fact that it had to face very serious difficulties in recruiting its professional staff, it succeeded in lending out over 300 million Islamic Dinars and in accumulating 18 million I.D. in interest revenues during the first fifteen months of its operations.

It appears also that Saudi Arabia, from the very beginning, had assumed a leading role in the bank's operations. The bank was established essentially at the initiative of the Saudi government. The Saudi government provided also the largest share of the bank's capital (23 percent), it enjoys the largest voting power on the board of governors, the president of the bank and chairman of the board of the executive directors is a former Saudi Deputy Minister of Education, the headquarters of the bank are located in

Jeddah, and the Saudi Arabian Monetary Agency acts as a depository and trustee of the bank.

The charter of the bank, as stated in the articles of agreement, and the first annual report seem to present a somewhat contradictory picture, as far as the guidelines for the lending policies of the bank are concerned. On the one hand, the articles state that the bank should always base its operations on sound, prudent financial and commercial considerations and should do everything possible to safeguard its capital and revenues. On the other hand, however, a strongly religious character of the bank is very forcefully emphasized also. It has been stated that its objectives include the fostering of economic welfare "on the basis of Islamic principles and ideals" and the promotion of "unity and solidarity of the Muslim world, in accordance with principles of the Shariah."[9] It remains to be seen to what extent the bank in its future operations will succeed in reconciling the sound financial considerations with the religious motivation and promotion of Muslim unity and solidarity.

As the bank has been in existence only since October 1975, and as it published only one report, covering the period of 1975 and 1976, a thorough evaluation of the bank cannot be made at this time. Nevertheless, the available data permit the formulation of several tentative conclusions.[10] The start of the bank was very promising and it launched its operations without undue delay. It appears also that most of the activities will be concentrated in providing loans based on sound financial grounds, rather than in offering grants based on economic or social needs of the recipients. The articles provide that grants can be made only from the resources of the Special Fund, which consists of the surplus revenue accumulated by the bank. Finally, the leading role of Saudi Arabia in the operations of the bank is unquestionable and decisive.

Since the official opening of the operations in October

1975, the bank has been very anxious to launch a large-scale program. In order to accelerate its involvement in various projects, the bank decided to move in the direction of joint-financing arrangements with other lenders. Its decision was based on a strong belief that a joint-financing arrangement is the most beneficial from the point of view of both the lenders and the borrowers. At the same time, the bank prepared a comprehensive document covering the entire field of its operations and declaring its policies and procedures.[11] This document, which could be compared to an investment prospectus, describes in a rather detailed way the conditions under which the bank will offer loans, the specific areas of economic activities that will interest the bank, and finally the limitations and restrictions that may be placed upon the prospective borrowers.

The second purpose of that document was to invite the prospective borrowers to submit their applications for loans. What the bank was attempting to do was to provide itself with a pipeline of projects that could be considered in the immediate future. In response to this invitation, over 150 applications were submitted by nineteen countries. In terms of sectoral division, forty-four projects related to transportation and communication sector, thirty-four to industry, thirty-four to agriculture, twenty-one to education, and the balance to public utilities. Most of the projects were submitted by various governmental agencies; the number of applications presented by the private sector was rather small. There were also several inquiries submitted by various international financial institutions interested in co-financing.

In deciding on the choice of the first projects to be financed by its resources, the bank placed a high priority on the projects submitted by the relatively undeveloped countries that have indicated their strong commitment to their own development by formulating comprehensive development plans. From this decision of the bank, it could be concluded that the bank has decided to place much stronger emphasis on the governmental plans and programs than on private, entrepreneurial initiative.

Some of the major financial commitments of the bank in its first year of operations included a loan of 6 million I.D. to the Song Loulou Hydro Electric Project in Cameroon, and a loan of 7 million I.D. to Jordan Petroleum Refining Company. In the first project the bank acted jointly with the Saudi Development Fund and the Kuwait Fund for Arab Economic and Social Development, while the financing of the Jordanian project was based on cooperation with the Arab Investment Company in Riyadh and the Arab Bank in Amman.

In the second year of its operation, the bank was planning to concentrate on two specific tasks: first, to provide a flow of funds in the form of grants to Moslem communities in the nonmember countries, and second, to participate in those projects that offer the best opportunity for an increased economic cooperation between the member countries. In addition, the bank was planning to place special emphasis on developing foreign trade facilities between the member countries and on increasing the transfer of technology.

Notes

1. Islamic Development Bank, *The First Annual Report 1975–1976*.
2. Ibid.
3. Islamic Development Bank, *Articles of Agreement (1977)*.
4. Ibid.
5. I.D.B., *First Annual Report*.
6. Ibid., p. 4.
7. Ibid., p. 9.
8. Ibid., p. 20.
9. Ibid., p. 25.
10. UNCTAD, *Financial Co-operation among Developing Countries* (TD/B/AC.19/R.8/Add.1), October 1975, pp. 84–87.
11. I.D.B., *First Annual Report*, p. 23.

8
The OPEC Special Fund

Although the membership in the Special Fund of the OPEC includes all member countries of the Organization of the Petroleum Exporting Countries, nevertheless, as the Arab members contribute over 55 percent of the financial resources of the Special Fund, the discussion of the fund is presented here. The non-Arab members of OPEC (Ecuador, Gabon, Indonesia, Iran, Nigeria, and Venezuela) contributed in 1976 approximately 45 percent of the fund's resources.[1] Major contributions were made by Iran ($220 million), Venezuela ($122 million), and Nigeria ($52 million). Gabon, Ecuador, and Indonesia made contributions of only $1 million each.

The initiative for the establishment of the Special Fund originated with the Shah of Iran. In 1974, the Shah proposed to form a new international financial institution to be financed jointly by OPEC members and OECD countries, and providing assistance to the development of the Third World nations.[2]

However, the response to the Shah's plan was not very encouraging. Subsequently, at the meeting held in Algiers in March 1975, the heads of states of the OPEC countries continued their discussion of creating a special facility aimed at providing financial aid to the developing countries. Several plans were presented for the consideration of the heads of states, and finally the draft proposals presented by

131

Saudi Arabia and Kuwait were chosen as a basis for the formation of the Special Fund. The principal objective of the Special Fund was to provide funds for economic development of all developing countries, excluding the members of OPEC.

The formal agreement creating the Special Fund stipulated that its resources should be utilized for providing financial aid on concessional terms, including long-term, interest-free loans to cover the deficits on the balance of payments, and to finance development programs and development projects.[3] The agreement establishing the Special Fund was signed in Paris on January 28, 1976.

All members of the OPEC became signatories of the agreement; but the effective participation of Ecuador and Iraq was delayed for several months. The resources originally committed to the Special Fund in 1976 totaled $800 million. The largest contributors to the fund were Iran, $200 million; Saudi Arabia, $205 million; Venezuela, $122 million; and Kuwait, $72 million. As mentioned earlier, the Arab members of OPEC contributed over 55 percent of the total resources of the Special Fund. Subsequently, in October 1976, the finance ministers of OPEC decided to contribute to the Special Fund their respective shares of profits resulting from the I.M.F. sales of gold. This contribution increased the resources of the fund by an additional $60 million. According to the agreement creating the fund, any member can increase its contribution to the Special Fund at any time. Also, a collective agreement of all members could decide to increase the contribution of all member countries. As indicated by Dr. Shihata, the present director-general, in technical terms the Special Fund is "an account collectively owned by the parties contributing to it . . . subject to the joint will of the owners, as expressed in the Agreement and in the resolutions of the Governing Committee."[4] Furthermore, the Special Fund is independent of any gov-

fer money directly to an agency appointed by the beneficiary country. Furthermore, it was expected that the Special Fund would engage mostly in co-financing with other institutions rather than assuming total responsibility for a complete financing of a project. It was believed that such an arrangement would expedite the processing of loans and eliminate the duplication of efforts. According to the director-general of the fund, Dr. Shihata, the sponsors wanted to avoid creating another agency duplicating the activities of many other similar institutions. He believed that "the proliferation of funds has often been listed as a weakness in the institutional framework of international financial assistance."[7]

The beneficiaries of the loans provided by the fund were limited to the governments of the developing countries and to "international development agencies, the beneficiaries of which are developing nations."[8] Such a definition would include most of the specialized agencies of the United Nations, and various intergovernmental, regional development agencies.

It was also decided that the resources of the fund should be used (1) to finance balance of payments deficits, (2) to finance specific programs and projects, and (3) to make contributions to the international agencies concerned with economic development.

According to the agreement establishing the fund, in addition to receiving applications for loans, the Special Fund could also invite the prospective beneficiaries to present their applications, following specific, predesigned programs and conditions. Actually, almost all of the financial assistance granted in 1976 was based on those predesigned programs. One program was aimed at the development of agriculture, and the other program was focused on the balance of payments assistance to the "Most Seriously Affected" countries. The MSA support program was offered under the following conditions: no interest charge, five-year period of grace, repayment in twenty years, and a service charge of 0.5 percent on funds actually withdrawn from the fund's loans.[9]

All loans were granted, and were to be repaid, in U.S. dollars, or in any freely convertible currency acceptable to the fund.

In the MSA balance of payments support program, the borrowing country was requested to deposit in the Special Fund's account an equivalent amount of local currency to finance additional, local development projects, approved jointly by the borrowing country and the Special Fund. The proceeds of the original loans granted by the Special Fund could be spent in any way, at the discretion of the borrower, as long as they were used for purposes specified in the loan agreement; they were not tied to any specific procurement of goods from any specific source. In general, the supervision of the implementation of the projects financed by the fund was placed in the various agencies of the United Nations, or similar international or interregional governmental agencies. The Special Fund did not intend to get directly involved in supervisory activities.

The Special Fund became operational on August 1, 1976; thus the first fiscal year covers the period August 1, 1976– July 31, 1977.[10] During that period the activities of the fund concentrated on two major projects: (1) a contribution of $400 million to the International Fund for Agricultural Development, and (2) balance of payments support program for the "Most Seriously Affected" countries.

The Governing Committee of the Special Fund authorized at its first meeting (May 10–12, 1976) a contribution of $400 million to the IFAD.[11] All member countries of the Special Fund contributed to this project, with Saudi Arabia and Iran providing over 50 percent of the total finances. This contribution of $400 million to the IFAD was made conditional on the contribution of at least $600 million by the OECD countries. The total starting budget of the IFAD was therefore to be equal to one billion dollars. The principal objective of the IFAD was to increase the production of food in Third World countries. The director general of the Special Fund was appointed as one member of the IFAD commission, and the OPEC countries were allocated one-third of the voting power in the governing bodies of the IFAD.

The allocation to the MSA balance of payments support program in 1976 amounted to $200 million. The objective of this program was to provide general support to cover the deficits on the balance of payments of the MSA nations. The definition of the MSA countries was based on the United Nations Assembly Resolution 3262. It defined them as "those which are at the greatest disadvantage in the world economy; the least developed, the landlocked and other low-income developing countries as well as others . . . whose economies have been seriously dislocated as the result of the present economic crisis, natural calamities, and foreign aggression and occupation."[12]

According to that definition, forty-five countries were classified under this category. They included most of the African nations, and also some of the most populous countries, such as India, Pakistan, Bangladesh, and Sri Lanka. They represented a total population of over one billion with an average annual per capita income below $200. The list included twenty-eight African countries, twelve Asian, and five Latin American. It covered the most densely populated developing countries, and also those classified by the United Nations as the "least developed countries" and as "food priorities countries."

On the basis of the definition and classifications provided by the United Nations, allocations from the Special Fund were made to forty-nine countries, between December 1976 and May 1977.[13] The total amount of $200 million was spent. The largest recipients were India and Pakistan (approximately $22 million each) and Bangladesh and Egypt (approximately $14 million each). Those four countries received, therefore, more than one-third of the total allocation. An average size of a loan for each remaining country was less than $3 million.

In addition to committing most of its resources to those two large-scale operations, the Special Fund engaged also in the first year of its operations in several other activities, jointly with several specialized agencies of the United Nations. According to the director general of the fund, Dr. Shihata, the primary objectives of those activities were to concentrate on providing assistance to the poorest sectors of the population in the recipient countries, especially in rural areas.[14] As a general goal, the fund attempted to decrease the dependence on foreign technology and to develop self-reliance by training programs and the development of labor-intensive technology.

At a meeting held by the finance ministers of the OPEC in Manila, on October 6, 1976, it was decided to transfer to the Special Fund the profits that each country would receive from the sale of gold held by the I.M.F.[15] It was expected that this transaction would increase the reserves of the fund by about $60 million. It was anticipated that eventually this amount would be contributed by the Special Fund to the I.M.F. Trust Fund and be used as financial aid to the developing countries.

The fund opened the second year of its operations with the fifth session of the governing committee, held August 2–3, 1977, in Vienna. At that session the committee approved the fund's participation in the financing of fourteen development projects in thirteen countries.[16] The total amount of loans for those fourteen projects equaled $54 million, while the total cost of the projects concerned was over one billion dollars, and was jointly covered by a large number of various international development agencies. The participation of the Special Fund amounted therefore to about 5 percent of the total cost of those projects. The three largest projects financed by the fund's loans included $11 million for a fertilizer plant in Pakistan, $8 million for the development of highways in the Philippines, and $7 million for a rural electrification program in Thailand.

The committee considered also several applications from the recipients of the fund's loans in the past, to use the local-currency counterpart funds of those loans for financing development activities in their countries. The committee approved the use of those funds, equivalent to $65 million, for twenty-one projects in nine countries. The two largest projects were thermal power stations in India ($22 million) and construction of transmission lines in Pakistan ($13 million).[17]

On September 30, 1977, the committee also approved a grant of $20 million to the U.N. Development Program activities in various parts of the world.[18] Initially, $12.7 million would be used for four regional development projects: an energy program in Central America, development of the Niger River basin in West Africa, offshore prospecting in East Africa, and the Red Sea–Gulf of Aden development plan. The allocation of the balance of $7.3 million was left for future decisions.

The sixth meeting of the governing committee of the Special Fund took place in Kuwait November 16–17.[19] The committee approved the participation of the fund in financing nine development projects in eight countries. The total loans provided by the fund amounted to $36.5 million. The largest project, involving $14 million, was the Off-Shore Development Plan in Bombay (India), and a loan of $8 million to the Industrial Development Bank in Egypt. The remaining loans averaged about $2 million each. The committee also approved the use of the local-currency counter-part funds for nine projects in six countries, totaling $7.5 million.

The original agreement creating the Special Fund envisaged the possibility that the fund might be liquidated once the initial resources of $800 million were distributed to the developing countries.[20] However, before the expiration of the first fiscal year, the conference of the OPEC ministers held in Doha December 15–17, 1976, decided that the fund should operate as a permanent institution. This decision was confirmed by the Special Meeting of the Ministerial Committee on Financial and Monetary Matters (Vienna, March 1, 1977), and an additional allocation of $800 million for the second fiscal year, starting in August 1977, was approved.[21]

All indications, therefore, seem to point out that the Special Fund, originally planned as a temporary arrangement, will develop into a permanent institution, making a significant contribution to the economic development of the Third World. There are several very definite characteristic features of the Special Fund that are very different from the usual features of many similar institutions. First, the Special Fund has very broad rules concerning its lending policies. It is not limited to project financing but it can also lend for balance of payments deficit financing, and furthermore it can contribute to various international agencies dealing with development. Second, the Special Fund attempts to maximize the utilization of the services of various international, interregional, and regional agencies that have professional competence in appraising, evaluating, and supervising the implementation of various projects. The operation of the Special Fund is very closely tied with many United Nations agencies that have been in existence for many decades and have proven their technical and professional expertise on numerous occasions. Finally, the Special Fund is characterized by a very marked concern for swift action. The agreement creating the fund was signed on January 28, 1976; it became effective on May 10, and the fund became operational on August 1. Before the end of August, more than three-fourths of the fund's resources were committed in principle. Thus, the implementation of the idea of creating the fund and putting it in operation took only several months; in many other instances a similar operation took several years. In conclusion, it could be stated that there are two very definite features characterizing the Special Fund, namely, simplicity and speed of operation.

In addition to the activities of the Special Fund described in detail in the preceding sections, the fund started in 1976, and intended to develop further in the subsequent years, a plan that would place it as a coordinating agency between various Arab funds, national and multilateral, engaged in providing financial assistance to the developing nations of the Third World. In 1976–77 fiscal year, this plan was only in the initial stages of its implementation. It resulted nonetheless in establishing close working relations with the African Development Bank, the Asian Development ment Bank, the Islamic Development Bank, and several Arab Development Funds. The Special Fund was also granted a status of an official observer with the I.M.F., the I.B.R.D., UNIDO, UNCTAD, and OECD.[22]

It is believed that in the long run the function of being the focus of the Arab effort to help financing the development of the Third World nations may prove to be one of the most significant and most successful activities of the fund. As mentioned elsewhere in this study, there exists at the moment a large number of various national, regional, and interregional agencies engaged in assisting the financing of economic development. Unfortunately, in most cases the activities of those agencies are not coordinated at all, and there is very little cooperation among them. Such a situation prevails in the relations between those agencies on the worldwide scale, and also within the Arab world. Obviously the effect of such a lack of coordination and harmonization of efforts and plans is detrimental to the success of their operations. There exist numerous cases of duplications of efforts, waste of scarce financial and human resources, and occasionally of outright conflicts among various plans.

It is anticipated that the OPEC Special Fund will eventually succeed in establishing itself as a focal point and the center for collaboration and cooperation among the national and multinational Arab financial institutions contributing to provide financial aid to the developing nations. Such an outcome would be most beneficial to all parties concerned.

Dr. Shihata, the director-general of the OPEC Special Fund, firmly believes that "the OPEC Fund could develop into an accounting pool through which all the financial aid provided by the OPEC member countries might be channelled."[23]

Notes

1. The OPEC Special Fund, *First Annual Report 1976*, p. 26.
2. Ibid., p. 11.
3. OPEC Special Fund, *Agreement Establishing the OPEC Special Fund.*
4. Dr. I.F.I. Shihata, *The OPEC Special Fund* (October 1976), p. 2.
5. OPEC Special Fund, *First Annual Report,* pp. 13 ff.
6. Ibid., p. 14.
7. Dr. Shihata, *OPEC Special Fund,* p. 3.
8. OPEC Special Fund, *Basic Information* (December 1976), p. 3.
9. OPEC Special Fund, *First Annual Report,* p. 18.
10. Ibid.
11. Ibid., p. 15–17.
12. Ibid., p. 18.
13. Ibid., p. 22.
14. Dr. Shihata, *OPEC Special Fund,* p. 10–11.
15. OPEC Special Fund, *First Annual Report,* p. 23.
16. OPEC Special Fund, *Press Release 77/7,* August 1977.

9
Special Arab Fund for Africa (SAAFA)

Following the increase in the price of oil by OPEC in 1973, a large number of African oil-importing countries found themselves in extreme financial difficulties. The increase in expenditures on imports of oil and imports of fertilizers based on oil caused very serious problems on their balances of international payments. To alleviate this situation, the Organization of African Unity, headquartered in Addis Ababa and representing all African nations, called for a meeting with the representatives of the Arab League.[1]

A special Committee of Seven was appointed by the O.A.U. in order to negotiate with the exporters of oil a grant of financial assistance that would reduce the burden of the increased oil prices.

Upon the invitation of the Arab League, the ministers of the petroleum-exporting countries met with the Committee of Seven in Cairo, in June 1974. The oil exporters recognized the extreme financial difficulties confronting the African nations, and decided therefore to establish a Special Aid Fund that would offer loans at concessional rates and with extended maturity periods. Those loans were intended to be used as a general support for the balance of payments of the borrowing countries that were adversely affected by the new oil prices.

The administration of the Special Aid Fund was placed jointly in the hands of the executive secretary of the Organization of African Unity and the secretary general of the Arab League. Their main function was to identify the prospective borrowers and to decide on the amount of each loan. The total amount of capital available for lending was fixed at $200 million. All Arab oil-exporting countries agreed to contribute to the fund. The largest single contribution was provided by the government of Saudi Arabia ($40 million), while Iraq, Libya, and Kuwait contributed $30 million each. Other exporting countries contributed smaller amounts.

Following the meeting in Cairo in June 1974 that established the Special Aid Fund, a prolonged controversy developed between the creditor and the debtor nations within the fund. The African borrowing nations wanted the fund to be placed under the control of the Organization of African Unity, while the Arab creditor nations preferred the fund to be controlled by the Arab League. After numerous meetings, it was finally decided that the Arab League would direct the operations of the Special Aid Fund. In October 1974, at the Seventh Arab Summit Conference in Rabat, it was decided to extend the operations of the fund for another year (i.e., 1975), and each contributor to the fund in 1974 agreed also to contribute to the fund an identical amount of money for the 1975 fiscal year. It was also decided that the Arab League should continue to administer the operations of the fund. Officially, therefore, there is no separate administrative machinery to operate the fund. Its operations are totally within the functions of the Arab League.

In the summer of 1975, the council of the Arab League, following the requests presented by the secretary of the O.A.U., decided to extend indefinitely the operations of the fund and to establish it as a permanent institution. It was also decided to keep the annual flow of contributions at the same level of $200 million. The largest recipients of loans in 1974 were Ethiopia ($14 million), Tanzania ($14 million), Uganda ($11 million), Chad ($9 million), and Zambia ($6 million). In deciding on requests for loans, the members of the Arab League considered the following factors: (1) the share of oil in total imports, (2) the magnitude of the deficit on the balance of payments, (3) per capita income, (4) domestic production of petroleum, (5) availability of other sources of energy, and (6) political stability of the borrower. All loans were granted under the provision that no interest payment would be required and the maturity of each loan would extend for eight years, with three years of grace. Furthermore, the loans were to be repaid to the Arab Bank for Economic Development in Africa. Thus the repayments of loans would provide an additional source of capital for the bank. This capital could be then used for further loans to the African nations. At the same time, however, the Arab League members decided that no pressure would be exerted upon those borrowers who were unable, or would find it extremely difficult, to repay the loans. It was generally anticipated that most of the loans granted by the Special Aid Fund would eventually be turned into grants.

As mentioned before in this study, in the early part of 1976 the administration of the Special Fund was transferred from the offices of the Arab League in Cairo to the offices of the Arab Bank for Economic Development in Africa, located in Khartoum, Sudan. Since that time, the Special Aid Fund constitutes, for all practical purposes, an integral part of the operations of the Arab Bank.

Note

1. The data presented in this section are based on UNCTAD, *Financial Co-operation among Developing Nations* (TD/B/AC.19/R.8), October 1975; *Financial Co-operation among Developing Nations* (TD/B/AC.19/R.8/Add.1), October 1975, pp. 72–75; *Economic Co-operation among Developing Nations* (TD/192/Supp.1), March 1976; and *International Financial Co-operation for Development* (TD/188/Supp.1/Add.1) February 1976.

10
OAPEC Special Account for the Arab Petroleum-Importing Countries (SAAPIC)

The substantial increase in the prices of oil that took place in the winter 1973–74 placed many Arab oil-importing countries in serious difficulties with their balances of payments. At the request of the secretariat of the OAPEC, a special study was made, attempting to ascertain the extent of the difficulties and the extent of the corrective measures that would have to be taken in order to eliminate the balance of payments difficulties. On the basis of that study, a report was submitted to the council of ministers of OAPEC in June 1974.[1] After a relatively brief discussion, the council of ministers decided to allocate $80 million to the Arab oil-importing countries in order to reduce the deficits on their foreign trade balances. The sum of $80 million was to be placed on a special account, and the administration and the payments from this account were put in the hands of the Arab Fund for Economic and Special Development, located in Kuwait. The OAPEC Special Account should therefore not be considered as a separate new fund or a separate new institution dealing with the economic development. It is only a separate account managed by the AFESD and specifically designed to reduce the difficulties of certain Arab countries, following the increase in their expenditures on oil imports.

146

The council of ministers decided that the assistance should be in the form of interest-free loans, to be repaid in ten equal installments, starting at the end of a ten-year period of grace. It was also decided that the operation of this Special Account should continue indefinitely, but that the actual amount of money allocated to the account should be determined annually by the council of ministers.

The amounts contributed in 1974 to the Special Account by the oil-exporting countries were as follows:

Country	Millions of dollars
Algeria	5.000
Iraq	16.000
Libyan Arab Republic	15.939
Qatar	5.000
Saudi Arabia	14.820
United Arab Emirates	10.000
Total:	77.759

Subsequently, in January 1975, Saudi Arabia made an additional contribution that brought the total resources of the Special Account equal to $79 million. The council of ministers agreed also on the distribution from the account in the following way:

Country	Dollars
Yemen (South)	11,158,750
Mauritania	4,641,250
Morocco	8,097,500
Somalia	7,208,750
Sudan	37,031,250
Yemen (North)	10,862,500
Total:	79,000,000

In May 1975, the council of ministers again discussed the subject of the Special Account, and again it reaffirmed its previous decision that the account should operate indefinitely, and also, that the AFESD should continue to administer the distribution of the monies from the account, according to a specific formula agreed upon by the council of ministers.

Although the origins of the Special Account have been directly connected with the change in the price of oil, and the amounts allocated from the account to each country seemed to have been based to a large extent on the magnitude of the difficulties on the balance of payments caused by the increased price, nevertheless the Special Account could be considered simply as another form of development aid from the Arab oil-exporting countries to a group of oil-importing, developing countries. The spending of the funds allocated from the Special Account was not tied, either directly or indirectly, to any investment in the energy sector or in oil-saving installations. The allocations could be spent in any form or fashion that the recipient country decided upon; no restrictions were placed upon the recipients by the administrators of the Special Account. So far, there have been no official statements made by the recipient governments, indicating in detail how the money provided by the Special Account has been spent. It can be assumed that most likely the funds provided by the Special Account were placed in the general revenue fund of the receiving nations, and spent for the purposes decided by the governments concerned, including economic and social development.

Finally, it may be mentioned here again that a similar special fund, the Special Arab Aid Fund for Africa (SAAFA), was created by the members of OAPEC in order to provide assistance to Black African countries (see the preceding section of this study). The principal functions of SAAFA and of SAAPIC were identical, namely, to assist in overcoming the difficulties in paying higher prices for oil.

The difference between those two institutions focused only on the recipients of aid; SAAPIC was designed to help the Arab countries, while SAAFA was designed to help the sub-Saharan countries of Black Africa.

Note

1. Data presented in this section are based on UNCTAD, *Financial Co-operation among Developing Nations* (TD/B/AC.19/R.8), October, 1975; *Financial Co-operation among Developing Nations* (TD/B/AC.19/R.8/Add.1), October 1975, pp. 78–79, *International Financial Co-operation for Development* (TD/188/Supp.1/Add.1), February 1976; and *Economic Co-operation among Developing Nations* (TD/192/Supp.1), March 1976.

Conclusions

Following the quadrupling of oil prices in 1973, and the emergence of huge surpluses of petro-dollars since 1974, one of the questions frequently asked by economic and political experts, as well as by the general public, concerns the future prospects of the flow of the Arab aid to developing nations. Is Arab foreign aid a temporary phenomenon, resulting from a very special set of coincidental events, or is it a long-term trend that will remain a more or less permanent feature in the arena of international economic relations? Is the Arab aid based on solid, long-range economic foundations or is it largely based on temporary, transient political considerations? Will Arab aid leave a lasting impact or will it simply disappear without trace, like a proverbial drop of water on a hot desert sand?

Since 1974 many attempts were made, and continue to be made, to answer those questions. As the Arab aid program is entering its fifth year more studies and more surveys are being made, trying to provide answers to those intriguing questions.

Before an attempt is made here to evaluate and comment on some of the recent projections concerning the Arab foreign aid, there are several rather general elements that have to be taken under consideration.

Any prediction about the future is always faced with some uncertainty. Any prediction about a new and unexpected event, where many political, social, and economic issues converge, obviously increases the degree of this uncertainty. In spite of this limitation, it is believed that a number of statements concerning the Arab aid can be made, based on certain underlying assumptions.

There is no doubt that Arab foreign aid is very closely tied to the magnitude of the surpluses of the petro-dollars that the Arab oil-exporting countries will accumulate in the future. The size of those surpluses depends, of course, on the relation between the supply of dollars resulting from the sales of oil, and the demand for those dollars, resulting from the flow of expenditures made by the oil-exporting countries in Europe and in the U.S.A. Therefore, anything that is likely to affect the demand for and the supply of oil will have a direct impact on the volume of the surplus of the petro-dollars, and ultimately on the magnitude of Arab foreign aid.

As far as the demand for oil is concerned, it can be safely assumed that in the foreseeable future the trend is very definitely in the upward direction. In spite of many technological advances, no practical substitute for oil appears on the horizon, at least for the remaining decades of the present century. In spite of many attempts to conserve energy, or to maximize the use of alternative sources of energy, such as coal, solar energy, hydro-power, atomic energy, etc., there does not appear any reasonable chance to eliminate the dependence on oil as a major source of energy in our modern industrialized life. All studies and all investigations made by experts in many parts of the world clearly indicate a continuously rising demand for oil in the next two or three decades. Recently, for example, M.I.T. (Boston, Mass.) published a massive study prepared by a group of thirty-five international experts from fifteen countries, called "Energy: Global Prospects." The findings of this study were also confirmed by recent reports published by the U.S. State Department and by OECD. Those studies indicate that as the demand for oil will continue to increase "the supply of oil will fail to meet increasing demand, even if energy prices rise 50 percent in real terms above current level."[1]

The M.I.T. team of experts arrived at its assessment by analyzing current energy use and projecting then the demand for the next twenty years, using different assumptions for economic growth, energy prices, and governmental policies. Using those different assumptions, the M.I.T. group arrived at different scenarios, with the size of the prospective oil gaps varying from fifteen to twenty million barrels per day, and the gap showing up as early as 1981.

One of the key assumptions concerned the output of the Arabian peninsula. If the daily production of this area is kept at 13 million barrels, the gap would emerge in 1984. If the output is doubled to 26 million barrels per day, the emergence of the gap could be postponed until 1991, and if there is no ceiling on Arabian peninsula production, and the daily production is operating at maximum capacity, the gap would be postponed till 1997. Although there has been some criticism about the validity of the assumptions made by the M.I.T. group, the general indications definitely point in the direction of a gap between the demand and the supply of oil before the end of the twentieth century. Most experts would be inclined to agree that the gap may be postponed, but it is coming.

The total revenues originating from oil will depend, of course, not only on the demand for oil, but will depend also on the price policies pursued by OPEC members. Therefore, any prediction concerning the revenues has to be based on certain assumptions concerning the future trend of oil prices. The quadrupling of oil prices in 1973 was totally unexpected and unforeseen. It could happen again. It would be reasonable, however, to assume that for a number of good reasons, economic as well as political, a fourfold jump in prices will not take place in the immediate future. But it should be expected that the prices of oil will continue the upward trend and follow, in general, the overall inflationary tendency, increasing annually at an average rate of approximately 5 to 10 percent. With the demand for oil being extremely inelastic, it should be expected that the aggregate oil revenues will continue to increase at approximately the same rate, unless the price of oil makes an unexpected jump.

The accumulation of the surpluses of the petro-dollars is affected obviously not only by the flow of oil revenues, but also by the flows of expenditures by the oil-exporting countries. Based on the experience of the past four years (1974–77), a very definite trend in the volumes of those expenditures could be detected. All indications are pointing in the direction of rather rapidly increasing rate of spending by all Arab oil producing countries.

In the mid-1970s it was generally believed that due to the rapidly increasing expenditures on imports by the oil-exporting countries, the accumulation of the annual surpluses of the petro-dollars may proceed at a somewhat decreasing rate.

Following the events of 1973 and the sudden increase of revenues of OPEC members, numerous attempts were made to estimate the future trend of the surpluses. As expected, there were rather significant differences in the estimates. Several widely publicized estimates were made by some of the leading banks in the U.S.: the Morgan Guaranty Trust Company, the Irving Trust Company, and the First National City Bank of New York.[2] According to the Morgan Trust Company, the positive trade balance of OPEC members would disappear in 1978, and turn negative in 1979, creating a negative balance on the current account. Thus, the peak of the accumulated balances would be reached in 1978.

The estimate made by the First National Bank was only

slightly more optimistic. According to this estimate, the positive trade balance and the positive current account balance would continue till 1979, and turn negative in 1980. The difference between the Morgan Bank's estimate and that of the First National Bank was only one year.

The Irving Trust Company made actually two estimates, one based on the assumption that oil prices would continue their steady increase, and the second that was based on the assumption that in 1977 the oil prices would experience a break. The Irving conclusion reached under the first assumption was essentially identical with the conclusions of the First National, while under the second assumption the accumulation of the surpluses would already have stopped in 1978.

Looking at those 1975 predictions from the present point of view, at the time of this writing (August 1978), it can be clearly seen that they all proved to be overly pessimistic. They all expected a disappearence of any further surpluses in 1978 or 1979. However, this is not what actually took place. Undoubtedly, the annual surpluses are diminishing but at a much slower rate than expected by the Morgan, First National, or Irving banks. One of the most recent studies made by OECD in January 1978 calculated the OPEC surplus for 1977 at $40 billion, and projected a surplus of $35 billion for 1978.[3]

In March 1978, the Morgan Guaranty Trust Company revised its previous estimates and published its most recent predictions.[4] According to those calculations, the OPEC surplus for 1977 would be somewhat less than $40 billion and for 1978 it was estimated to equal $29 billion. If this estimate proved to be correct, it would mean that in one year the surplus would have been reduced by about 25 percent. If the reduction of the annual surpluses continued at the same rate for the next few years, the absolute amount of surpluses at the end of the present decade would shrink to about $18 billion per annum.

The topic of surpluses accumulated by the OPEC members was also analyzed by the well-known Wharton Economic Forecasting Conference held in Philadelphia, in June 1977.[5] There has been mounting concern that the rapid build-up of the international credit accumulated by OPEC members could topple the world financial system if it continues. According to Dr. R. de Vries, vice-president of the Morgan Guaranty, who attended that conference, the outlook is much more sanguine than frequently estimated. He believed that the annual surplus of OPEC would narrow to about $10 billion by the end of the decade, compared with the $35 billion to $40 billion annual total of the last two years, and the $67 billion accumulated in 1974 alone. His prediction was based mainly on Saudi Arabia's increasing ability to absorb more imports of goods and services to offset a large part of its massive oil earnings.

In May 1977, the International Monetary Fund completed a study of the flow of surpluses accumulated by the oil-exporting countries. I.M.F. director Johannes Whiteveen, commenting on this study, expressed his views that as "the oil-exporting countries are sharply increasing their imports while their exports earnings are restrained by the worldwide recession," the OPEC surplus would continue the downward trend and be expected to be slightly less than $40 billion in 1976, as compared with $67 billion in 1974.[6]

Mr. Mohammed Aba al-Khail, Minister of Finance and National Economy of Saudi Arabia, indicated at a news conference held in the spring of 1977 that "Saudi Arabia's capacity to spend money is increasing rapidly, raising the prospect that the Kingdom's outlays may match income in another year or two."[7] This would mean, of course, less Saudi money available for foreign lending. Commenting on the conditions of several major industrial projects undertaken in Saudi Arabia, he stated that "our absorption capacity is rising steadily because of such projects."[8] He also announced that during the fiscal year that ended June 27,

1976, Saudi Arabia spent $22 billion while its revenues totaled $28.7 billion. In the next year, which under Moslem calendar ended June 17, 1977, revenues were expected to increase to $31 billion, while expenditures were expected to hit $27 billion. Looking ahead to the fiscal year of 1978, Mr. al-Khail said "that gap should narrow further in 1978."[9]

The rapidly increasing capacity to absorb more imports by the economy of Saudi Arabia was also confirmed by the Economic Review presented by SAMA (Saudi Arabian Monetary Agency). It showed, for example, that "the value of imports in 1975 increased by 85 percent as compared with 1974, and were more than triple in value of 1973 and six times that in 1971. A large part of the total increase resulted from accelerated Government spending and rising private income levels."[10]

The topic of the surpluses of the petro-dollars accumulated by OPEC was the subject of an interview given by Mr. Mohammed Aba al-Khail, Minister of Finance and National Economy, and Mr. Abdel Aziz Quraishi, Governor of the Saudi Arabian Monetary Agency, to a group of foreign journalists.[11] The minister and the governor stated that these are temporary artificial surpluses that give a falsely sanguine picture of the kingdom's economic position. They also believed that the term "surplus" is not actually appropriate at all. "We don't have a surplus; we have a temporary liquidity,"[12] Mr. al-Khail said. He projected that "Saudi Arabia's expenditure would catch up with its income at the end of the decade and that monetary reserves may be used up by the end of the next decade, even allowing for increased oil production and continually rising prices."[13] Mr. Quraishi said that "Saudi Arabia is a developing country and needs every cent, if not now, then soon." According to Mr. al-Khail, "the costs of development are very high. Oil production is increasing but we believe the absorptive capacity is going up even faster. We can see the point where we will have to dip into the surpluses," concluded the minister.[14]

The problems associated with the surpluses of the OPEC and the growing deficits of the developing nations were subject of a recent study and investigation conducted by the United States Senate Foreign Relations Committee. It appears that a major difference of opinions developed between the committee and the administration. The Senate's study stated that "the massive accumulation of financial surplus by the oil exporting countries is not a temporary phenomenon but is a chronic, systematic imbalance in the international market place that jeopardizes the international financial system."[15]

Mr. Anthony Solomon, the Under-Secretary of the Treasury, however, when testifying before the committee, expressed the President's view that "OPEC surplus will disappear as the oil exporting nations build up their economies and their capacity to absorb imports." The senators disagreed with Mr. Solomon and voiced their deep concern about "the increasing problems that the developing nations are experiencing in meeting their debt obligations."[16] The senators saw a very close relationship between the mounting surpluses of the petro-dollars and the deepening deficits on the balances of payments of the developing nations. The Senate's study showed, for example, that the public external debt of the developing countries is estimated at 150 to 200 billion dollars, and "in aggregate the developing nations are spending 20 percent of their export earnings just to serve external debt."[17] The senators also quoted a study presented by the American Express Banking Company, showing that "one out of every four dollars borrowed by the developing nations in 1977 will go for debt servicing and that by 1980 one out of every two dollars will have to be used to repay old debts."[18] It seems, however, that the differences in opinion between the Senate and the administration have been essentially based on differences in emphasis. While the administration was looking at the OPEC's surpluses primarily from the point of view of the industrialized nations, the Senate was focusing its attention on the developing countries in Africa and Asia. The senators' concern seemed to be quite justified that the increasing capacity to absorb imports by OPEC members will not help the poor, underdeveloped countries at all, simply because they have very little to offer for export to the OPEC group.

It appears from numerous studies and reports that the issue of the growing propensity to import in the OPEC group is one of the crucial questions concerning the magnitudes of the surpluses, and therefore also the volume of the foreign assistance provided by the oil exporters to developing nations. One of the recent studies of this topic was presented by the *Middle East Year Book 1977*.[19] The study talks about the "expenditure explosion" taking place in the oil-exporting countries, and believes that this expenditure is "almost uncontainable." As the import expenditures are increasing faster than oil revenues do, the surpluses of the petro-dollars will continue to decline. What is causing this "expenditure explosion"?

An examination of the expenditure patterns in the past few years, and at the present, provides a clear-cut answer. A review of the national budgets of the major oil exporters, and of their national development plans, discloses rather clearly that the investment expenditures in the industrial sector represent a relatively minor part of the total investment flow. A much larger flow of investments is directed to the commercial sector, and even larger flow is channeled to investment in the social sector. While the capacity to absorb investments in the industrial sector in most developing countries is severely limited in the short run, the capacity to absorb investments in the social sector is virtually unlimited. Why? The answer is rather obvious: It is much easier to build schools, hospitals, clinics, streets, highways, etc., than to build and operate industrial installations. In addition, of course, to the investment expenditure in the social sector, there is always present a huge flow of expenditures for current consumption.

Such a pattern of expenditure indicates that the total return from the current flow of expenditures on investments is rather limited while the expenditures on investments in the social sector or on current consumption do not generate any monetary profit. Furthermore, for all practical purposes, the commitments to social consumption are unlimited.

A study of the current development plan of Saudi Arabia clearly demonstrates the expenditure pattern discussed above. While over 60 percent of the project budget goes to housing, health, and education, only 29 percent goes for the development of economic resources. Directly productive investments account for only 8 percent of the total investment expenditure. Similar patterns of expenditures could be also found in the Gulf countries. For example, the share of national budget allocated to housing, transport, and education increased between 1950 and 1972 from 10 percent to 70 percent in Bahrain, from 23 percent to 64 percent in Kuwait, and from 10 percent to 33 percent in Qatar.[20] Those figures prove rather conclusively that the expenditures in the social sector of the economy are increasing very rapidly and can absorb an almost unlimited amount of funds.

To add to this trend, one should also consider the problem of rising expectations of the society. No matter how substantial the progress has been in the recent past, the public's demand for better medical and educational services, better housing, and better transportation is invariably ahead of the available demand. A well-known saying that "appetite increases with eating" would find its perfect application in the demand for social services. Thus the opportunity for rapid increase in spending in the social sector is not only technically easy and feasible, but it is always stimulated by a rapidly increasing public demand. And, as the national expenditures are increasing, the surpluses of the available petro-dollars are shrinking. If the equally unsaturated demands for military expenditures are added to the never-ending demand for social consumption, the trend indicated above will obviously accelerate.

As the flows of expenditures seem to be characterized by an explosive increase, the surpluses of the petro-dollars will decline, and the opportunities to offer foreign aid will be reduced correspondingly. Projecting the expected flow of foreign aid into the future, the *Middle East Yearbook* believes that in mid-1980s only Saudi Arabia will have surpluses, because only in Saudi Arabia is the rate of new oil discoveries greater than the growth of the extraction rate. Already in 1977, according to the U.S. Senate study quoted in the preceding section, over 90 percent of the OPEC's surpluses were actually in the hands of only three countries, Saudi Arabia, Kuwait, and the U.A.E. The surpluses of all other OPEC members have, for all practical purposes, disappeared.

The preceding discussion focused largely on the estimates of the aggregate volume of surpluses of the petro-dollars and on the overall relations between the oil-exporting countries and the rest of the world in general. From the point of view of this study, however, the relations between the oil-exporting countries and the developing nations officially classified by the United Nations as LDC (less developed countries) or as MSA (most seriously affected) are of much greater interest.

As mentioned earlier, the relationship between OPEC and the aggregate balance of payments of the rest of the world has been changing rather significantly since 1973. The analysis conducted in aggregate terms does not, however, disclose certain fundamental differences between various groups of countries confronting OPEC. Specifically, it does not show the contrasting effects upon the industrialized nations, usually grouped within OECD, and the developing nations, usually referred to as LDCs or MSAs. The experience of the four years 1974–77 and the presently available data rather conclusively demonstrate that the position of OECD countries versus the OPEC is steadily strengthening while the position of the LDCs is equally steadily deteriorating further.

According to a study published by OECD in January 1978, the total deficit of OECD countries was estimated at $22 billion for 1978, down from $32 billion in 1977.[21] All OECD members, except the U.S. will show an improvement from $4.25 billion in 1977 to $3.75 billion in 1978, and of France from $3 billion in 1977 to $2 billion in 1978. At the same time Germany is expected to increase its surplus from $2.25 billion in 1977 to $3 billion in 1978, England from $750 million to $3.5 billion, and Italy from $1 billion to $1.75 billion.

At the same time, the Economics Ministry of Germany announced that in 1977 Germany posted its first-ever trade surplus with the OPEC.[22] According to a statement from the ministry, in 1977 Germany had a surplus of $1.6 billion with the OPEC group, compared with $3.6 billion deficit in 1976, and $13.3 billion deficit in 1974. Although Germany is only the first OECD country to show a trade surplus with OPEC, nevertheless the German experience may indicate a similar trend in other OECD countries. What has been primarily responsible for the German success in eliminating the payment gap with OPEC was the rapid increase in German exports to the OPEC group, while the import bill has remained virtually the same since 1974, at about DM 24 billion annually. According to the data published by the ministry, in 1974 the OPEC group accounted for only 4.5

percent of the total German exports. This percentage has increased to 7.5 percent in 1975, to 8 percent in 1976 and to 9.1 percent in 1977. In 1977, total German exports to OPEC equaled DM 25 billion while oil imports totaled only DM 24 billion. Thus a trade surplus emerged.

A report published by the Bank for International Settlements (BIS) in Basel, Switzerland, essentially confirmed the estimates made by the OECD study discussed above.[23] The BIS report stated that in the last quarter of 1977 the OPEC group became a net borrower of new funds from the international banking system. The OPEC group borrowed $2.2 billion in new funds, and deposited only $400 million, making the net borrowing equal to $1.8 billion. Overall, however, OPEC continued to be a major net source of funds for international lending. At the end of 1977, their total deposits equaled $73.1 billion and their borrowing $31.9 billion, leaving thus a net surplus position of $41.2 billion.

As mentioned above, Germany is only the first example of an OECD country having a trade surplus with OPEC. Nevertheless, this example indicates a general trend and underlines one of the fundamental issues that is strongly emphasized in this study, namely, that the import propensity of the OPEC is increasing very rapidly, and is also increasing at a much faster rate than the oil revenues. Thus, the annual surpluses of the petro-dollars are diminishing and at some future point in time may disappear completely. The analysis of the increasing propensity to import has been presented on the preceding pages of this study. What is attempted to be stressed here is the fact that the OECD countries as the principal exporters of the goods demanded by OPEC have the capacity, the initiative, and the opportunity to increase the speed of recycling of the petro-dollars, and thus to improve their relative position versus the OPEC group.

However, the situation of the LDCs is in a totally different category. On the one hand, their total imports have been increasing very rapidly, especially since 1974, while on the other hand their exports earnings have been increasing only very slowly. Thus the deficits on their balances of trade have been mounting. According to the data published by the I.M.F., the aggregate trade deficits of the LDCs increased from $23 billion in 1973 to $55 billion in 1974.[24] The situation of the LDCs has deteriorated not only in absolute terms but even more in relative terms. A study prepared by the I.B.R.D. entitled "Prospects for Developing Countries, 1976–1980" revealed that the share of the developing countries in world trade declined between 1970–74 from 2.3 percent to 1.4 percent, while at the same time the share of OPEC increased from 6.3 percent to 16.8 percent, a rate of increase of almost 300 percent.[25]

Within the LDC group the effects of the changing pattern of trade have not been equally distributed. Several countries in Latin America have experienced an increase in the prices of their export goods. Thus, the adverse impact of the higher oil prices was relatively small. Another group of countries, such as South Korea, Taiwan, Singapore, and Hong Kong, were able to increase substantially their exports to OPEC, and by doing so they had the opportunity to recycle their petro-dollars. Finally, the third group of the LDCs that was exposed to the maximum adverse impact consists of some forty nations in tropical Africa and South Asia, with a combined population of over one billion. Those nations, at the moment and in the foreseeable future, do not seem to have any chance to counteract the adverse effects of the new prices of oil. Those nations, classified by the United Nations as MSA, have exceedingly poor prospects for the future as far as their economic growth is concerned.[26]

The continuing increase in the oil-imports bill of the

LDCs is simply due to the fact that they are much more dependent on oil as an energy source than the OECD countries. Furthermore, the share of oil imports in the total imports is much higher for the LDCs than it is for the OECD countries. Thus the impact of the increase in the prices of oil was much heavier on the LDCs than it was on the industrialized nations of Europe. For example, in India in 1975, the cost of oil imports represented 25 percent of the total import expenditures. In many countries in tropical Africa, the relations between oil imports and total imports is of similar magnitude.[27]

While the import expenditures of the LDCs have been increasing rather rapidly, primarily as the result of higher oil prices, their export revenues have remained essentially stagnant in the past few years. There are two elements that can account for this unsatisfactory situation. In the first place the LDCs have very little to export in general, and in the second place the prices of their exportable commodities, mostly primary commodities, have suffered a general decline since the late 1960s. This decline continued in most cases through the 1970s.

Therefore, the 1973 increase in oil prices had, and continues to have, a much greater impact on the balances of payments of the LDCs than on the balances of payments of the OECD countries. According to data provided by the United Nations, the 1974 deficits of the LDCs were, in aggregate, equal to about 50 percent of their combined export earnings, while in the OECD countries those deficits equaled only 10 percent of their export earnings.[28]

Since 1974 the situation of the LDCs has been gradually deteriorating, and they have become increasingly more dependent on borrowing from abroad and on foreign aid programs offered by European or Arab countries.[29] However, according to the *Middle East Yearbook 1977* it is generally believed that "in spite of OPEC aid, rising oil prices have dealt a severe blow to the development prospects of the Third World countries.''[30] In order to reduce the adverse impact of the increased oil prices and to provide assistance to the development plans of the developing nations in general, the Arab countries have launched their foreign aid programs.

There is no doubt that the magnitude of those programs is very impressive, when measured in terms of dollars. An amount of over $6 billion per annum represents a significant volume of purchasing power by any standard.

In addition to calculating and discussing the Arab aid in absolute terms, an examination of this aid in relative terms would be equally or even more interesting and impressive. The discussion of the aid in relative terms could be approached from two different points of view, first, relative to the size of the Arab economies, and second, relative to the needs of the developing countries, the recipients of the aid.

As the detailed analyses presented in the preceding sections of this study have revealed, when the aid is analyzed from the point of view of the donor countries, it would be a gross understatement to say that its magnitude is substantial and significant. As a matter of fact it is almost overwhelming. There is no precedence in the whole economic history presenting a situation where a nation or a group of nations offered 6 or 8 or 10 percent of their G.N.P. in assistance to foreign nations. In terms of effort and real sacrifice, the Arab aid is unparalleled in history. The generosity of this aid is further magnified when it is considered that until very recently most of the donor nations were among the underdeveloped nations, and even today, in spite of their present wealth, still should be classified as developing rather than developed nations.

Parenthetically, the size of the Arab effort should be compared with the dimensions of the foreign aid provided by OECD countries. Only in the instances of one or two countries, on one or two occasions, has foreign aid reached one percent of the G.N.P. of the OECD nations. In most cases, the share of the G.N.P. offered in foreign aid equaled approximately one-half of one percent.

The relative magnitude of the effort becomes more apparent when more specific comparisons are made. For example, the aid provided by Saudi Arabia alone, a country in the initial stages of development with a population of about 7 million, is approaching very closely the size of the economic aid provided presently by the United States, a country in the most advanced stage of economic development, with a population of over 200 million people.

Thus, Arab foreign aid, whether measured in absolute terms or in relation to the sacrifices of the donor nations, presents a most impressive and striking picture.

But the final question remains: What is the size of this aid in relation to the needs of the recipients? Will Arab aid leave a permanent and decisive impact upon the economies of African and Asian nations? Unfortunately, the answer, in the opinion of this author, has to be rather negative. There are several reasons that could account for such a conclusion.

Although the size of flow of Arab funds to the African and Asian nations is very impressive, nonetheless this flow does not even come close to compensating those nations for their increased expenditures on imports of oil and other products, such as fertilizers and insecticides, based on petrochemicals.[31] As mentioned in the preceding parts of this study, the demand for oil, especially by the developing nations, is very inelastic. Therefore, the 400-percent increase in the price of oil that took place in 1973 resulted in many instances in increased import expenditures by a similar percentage. To this direct effect of higher prices for oil one has to add the effects of higher prices of many other products based on petrochemicals, which experienced a similar increase and which are imported by the developing nations.

The aggregate volume of Arab financial aid amounts to between $6 billion and $8 billion per annum. As stated above, this is a very substantial amount of money. Yet how much of it is reaching the developing nations of Africa and Asia? The available data very clearly indicate that in the past few years between two-thirds and three-fourths of this aid was directed to three countries only, namely, Egypt, Jordan, and Syria. All the other countries in Africa and Asia had to share only one-third or one-fourth of the aggregate amount. In terms of actual dollars, that would amount to approximately $2 billion per annum, shared by more than fifty countries in Africa and South Asia.

Finally, when the overall situation of Africa and South Asia, especially India, Pakistan, and Bangladesh, is considered, the picture that emerges is not very encouraging at all. Almost all recent studies conducted by the OECD, the various agencies of the United Nations, or by independent experts indicate that the development prospects for those countries in the foreseeable future are rather gloomy. There are many reasons that contribute to such a conclusion.

The rapidly increasing populations in Africa and in the already overpopulated countries such as India and Bangladesh preclude the possibility of any real growth. In the past few years, the rate of population growth was essentially the same as the rate of growth in the real G.N.P. Thus, the real output per capita has been virtually stagnant.[32] Furthermore, the demand for the primary commodities exported by those countries has been declining in relation to the rapidly increasing demand for the industrial products produced by the industrialized nations. Their rate of participation in the world trade has shown a steadily declining trend. While the Indian subcontinent has been facing the seemingly insoluble problems of overpopulation, the African continent has been faced with the equally insoluble problems of lack of unity and political fragmentation. Most of the African countries are simply too small to offer a viable basis for industrial development and for economic progress. In spite of strenuous and constant efforts of the United Nations agencies, the political and economic fragmentation of Africa continues. And, finally, the lack of political and social stability and the frequent military conflicts and political tensions surely do not contribute to a rapid rate of growth or economic well-being.

It seems that in spite of great efforts and generosity of the Arab nations, the flow of the Arab aid will not very likely have any significant and durable impact upon the economies of the recipient nations. Undoubtedly it will help them in the short run to overcome the economic difficulties and to alleviate human misery and suffering, but it is rather unlikely to leave any decisive impact upon the path of their future development in the twentieth century.

Such a conclusion should not be really surprising at all. Similar conclusions have been reached in the past concerning foreign aid provided by other countries. The Agency for International Development of the United States, for example, already in the mid 1960s had changed completely its approach to economic aid and has adopted a new policy toward the distribution of its aid. Instead of distributing the financial assistance in relatively small quantities to a large number of countries, the agency has decided to limit drastically the number of recipients and to concentrate the flow of its aid to a selected, small group of countries that would offer the best prospects for economic development. Thus, on each continent only two or three countries were chosen as prospective targets for aid that, it was believed, could lead to a substantial economic growth, while the aid to all other nations would continue in limited quantities only, on purely humanitarian grounds.

Apparently, the facts behind such a decision were based

on the belief that economic development can take place only if generated by the dynamic forces within the society itself and by its own sacrifices, effort, and determination to make it successful. Foreign aid and other stimulation from outside obviously may help this process, but it can never be used as a substitute for the indigenous effort and for the willingness to bear sacrifices in order to attain certain objectives.

The preceding discussion of the future trends of the Arab aid primarily emphasized economic considerations. When looked at from the economic point of view, there are numerous indications strongly suggesting that the flow of the Arab aid to developing nations has already passed its peak and shows a downward tendency at this time. This gradual reduction stems primarily from the fact that the surpluses of petro-dollars are shrinking, mainly due to the increasing propensity to import by oil-exporting countries. Almost all experts are inclined to agree that, when looking beyond the year of 1980, only Saudi Arabia and Kuwait will have any significant surpluses of petro-dollars.[33] The fact, however, that the surpluses of petro-dollars are diminishing does not necessarily mean that Arab foreign aid will cease to flow. As mentioned earlier, Arab foreign aid was motivated not only by economic considerations but also by political, social, and purely humanitarian aspects. Therefore, even if the justification for aid may be somewhat reduced on purely economic grounds, nonetheless there may still exist some valid and compelling arguments based on political considerations that will justify the continuation of the aid.

Although in the past, a major portion of the Arab foreign aid was in the form of loans based on economic considerations, there are numerous indications at the moment that most of those loans may not be repaid at all and that they should be considered as grants. The overall economic situation of the African nations has reached such a critical stage that they are requesting the lenders to write off the outstanding debt.

At a recent meeting of the executive council of UNCTAD attended by the representatives of over 100 nations, a request was formally presented that the loans granted in the past be considered as grants.[34] Apparently, the total debt of the LDCs has reached the amount of over $250 billion, and there does not appear to exist any reasonable chance that the LDCs could ever repay it. Already now over 20 percent of their total export earnings are allocated to the payment of interest on this debt. So far only four countries have agreed to write off their debts: Norway, Holland, West Germany, and England. What will be the attitude of the Arab countries when a request is made directly to them to write off the outstanding loans?

It is possible that the Arab foreign aid will evolve in a way similar to the American foreign aid. The U.S. foreign assistance program, launched in the late 1940s, started in the form of the Marshall Plan as a temporary phenomenon, based primarily on the economic considerations, to assist in the postwar economic reconstruction of Europe. Over the past three decades, however, U.S. aid has acquired more and more a political aspect and has been transformed into one of the major tools of American foreign policy and has become a permanent feature of the national budget. It is conceivable that Arab aid may also undergo a similar transformation and gradually become a permanent feature in the international relations between the Arab and developing nations in Africa and Asia.

Notes

1. "Oil: A Looming Gap," *Newsweek,* 23 May 1977, p. 41.

2. Yoon S. Park, *Oil Money and the World Economy* (Boulder, Colo.: Westview Press, 1976), pp. 48–50.

3. "OECD Warns of New Dollar Woes," *International Herald Tribune*, 14 February 1978.

4. "OPEC Surplus," *Saudi Gazette*, 4 March 1978.

5. "Bank Aide Sees Reduction in Payments Imbalances," *International Herald Tribune*, 15 June 1977.

6. "OPEC 13 Put More of Surplus into Foreign Investment, Aid," *International Herald Tribune*, 13 May 1977.

7. "Riyadh Reported Narrowing Gap between Income, Outlay," *International Herald Tribune*, 29 April 1977.

8. Ibid.

9. Ibid.

10. "$7.7 bn. Imports to Kingdom," *Saudi Gazette*, 24 February 1977.

11. "Two Saudi Finance Aides See a Wealth of Economic Woes," *International Herald Tribune*, 30 May 1977.

12. Ibid.

13. Ibid.

14. Ibid.

15. "Senate Staff Study Critical of Mounting Oil Debt," *International Herald Tribune*, 20 September 1977.

16. Ibid.

17. Ibid.

18. Ibid.

19. *Middle East Yearbook 1977*.

20. Ibid., p. 73.

21. "OECD Warns of New Dollar Woes," *International Herald Tribune*, 14 February 1978.

22. "West Germany in Surplus in Trade With OPEC," *International Herald Tribune*, 10 February 1978.

23. "Countries in OPEC Become Net Borrowers," *International Herald Tribune*, 9 February 1978.

24. Yoon S. Park, *Oil Money and the World Economy*, p. 122.

25. Ibid., p. 154.

26. "World Economic Forecast," *Newsweek*, 26 September 1977.

27. Yoon S. Park, *Oil Money and the World Economy*, p. 60.

28. "World Economic Forecast," *Newsweek*, 26 September 1977.

29. UNCTAD, *Recent Trends in International Trade and Development* (TD/186), May 1976, p. 9.

30. *Middle East Yearbook 1977*, p. 20.

31. UNCTAD (TD/186), p. 20.

32. "World Economic Forecast," *Newsweek*, 26 September 1977.

33. "Spent Petrodollars," *Arabia and the Gulf* 1, no. 10 (6 June 1977).

34. "West Agrees to Look at Debt Aid for Poorest," *Saudi Gazette*, 11 March 1978.

APPENDIX—TABLES

List of Tables

1. Total Net Flows from Arab Countries
2. Nonconcessional Assistance in 1976
3. Concessional Assistance in 1976
4. G.N.P. at Current Market Prices
5. Financial Flows (DAC Members)
6. Financial Flows (DAC Members)
7. Shares in Total World Exports
8. Balance of Payments (non-oil developing countries)
9. Current-Account Balances for Major Regions

173

Table 1.
Total Net Flows from Arab Countries to Developing Countries

Donor Country	$ million				As percent of G.N.P.			
	1973	1974	1975	1976	1973	1974	1975	1976
Iraq	11.1	440.2	251.4	119.7	0.21	4.16	1.91	0.75
Kuwait	550.0	1,250.1	1,711.2	1,874.8	9.17	11.46	11.44	11.50
Libya	403.7	263.2	362.8	373.2	6.25	2.21	2.96	2.43
Qatar	93.7	217.9	366.7	245.4	15.62	10.90	16.90	10.37
Saudi Arabia	334.9	1,622.1	2,466.7	2,826.0	4.12	7.19	7.42	7.04
U.A.E.	288.6	749.4	1,206.6	1,143.8	12.03	9.78	13.59	11.45
TOTAL	1,682.0	4,542.9	6,365.4	6,582.9	5.85	6.92	7.41	6.57

Source: OECD, *Flows of Resources from OPEC Members to Developing Countries* (Statistical Tables), 1977.

Table 2.
Nonconcessional Assistance in 1976

$ million

Donor Country	Commitments			Net Disbursements		
	Bilateral	Multilateral	Total	Bilateral	Multilateral	Total
Iraq	4.0	——	4.0	——	23.0	23.0
Kuwait	1347.1	876.4	2223.5	1076.9	271.0	1347.9
Libya	16.1	38.3	54.4	218.3	51.3	269.6
Qatar	7.4	200.6	208.0	22.6	47.7	70.3
Saudi Arabia	220.5	1163.5	1384.0	49.3	460.9	510.2
U.A.E.	53.1	319.9	373.0	29.6	92.3	121.9
TOTAL	1648.2	2598.7	4246.9	1396.7	946.2	2342.9

Source: OECD, Flows of Resources from OPEC Members to Developing Countries (Statistical Tables), 1977.

Table 3.
Concessional Assistance in 1976

$ million

Donor Country	Commitments			Net Disbursements		
	Bilateral	Multilateral	Total	Bilateral	Multilateral	Total
Iraq	97.2	84.1	181.3	49.3	47.4	96.7
Kuwait	544.7	210.8	755.5	376.3	150.6	526.9
Libya	91.3	125.9	217.2	27.6	76.0	103.6
Qatar	99.6	38.7	138.3	144.0	31.1	175.1
Saudi Arabia	2,415.1	387.5	2,802.6	2,073.7	242.1	2,315.8
U.A.E.	1,085.6	95.8	1,181.4	968.5	53.4	1,021.9
TOTAL	4,333.5	942.8	5,276.3	3,639.4	600.6	4,240.0

Source: OECD, Flows of Resources from OPEC Members to Developing Countries (Statistical Tables), 1977.

Table 4.
G.N.P. at Current Market Prices

$ million

Countries	1973	1974	1975	1976
Iraq	5,300	10,591	13,195	15,997
Kuwait	5,998	10,904	14,959	16,300
Libya	6,459	11,912	12,242	15,372
Qatar	600	2,000	2,170	2,366
Saudi Arabia	8,130	22,565	33,225	40,133
U.A.E.	2,400	7,661	8,876	9,990
TOTAL	28,887	65,633	84,667	100,158

Source: OECD, Flows of Resources from OPEC Members to Developing Countries (Statistical Tables), 1977.

Table 5.
Financial Flows

Official development assistance of DAC member countries, net disbursements, 1969–1973
(Millions of Dollars)

Country	Bilateral[a]			Contributions to multi-lateral institutions[b]			TOTAL		
	1969	1971	1973	1969	1971	1973	1969	1971	1973
Australia	158.2	190.9	262.8	16.4	11.2	23.0	174.6	202.1	285.8
Austria	4.6	6.7	7.9	8.6	5.7	32.5	13.2	12.4	40.4
Belgium	82.9	109.1	177.2	31.2	35.9	55.9	114.1	145.0	233.1
Canada	159.7	289.3	344.1	85.0	96.5	165.5	244.7	385.8	509.6
Denmark	30.9	36.0	70.6	23.4	38.0	59.9	54.3	74.0	130.5
France	826.2	925.0	1293.0	95.2	128.7	194.1	921.4	1053.7	1487.3
Germany, Federal Republic of	382.5	507.7	654.0	127.8	204.7	310.6	510.3	712.4	964.6
Italy	54.5	109.5	79.2	24.6	45.6	73.8	79.1	155.1	153.0
Japan	337.1	432.8	742.5	95.9	78.7	245.8	433.0	511.5	988.3
Netherlands	103.1	150.8	220.0	38.3	63.8	92.1	141.4	214.6	312.1
New Zealand[c]	—	—	19.3	—	—	7.1	11.6	16.7	26.4
Norway	12.9	18.2	40.6	16.1	24.2	46.2	29.0	42.4	86.8
Portugal	69.8	98.4	61.1	0.4	0.4	0.5	70.2	98.8	61.6
Sweden	54.3	65.4	153.1	65.7	91.2	122.0	120.0	156.6	275.3
Switzerland	17.2	20.1	33.3	12.0	9.0	31.7	29.2	29.1	65.0
United Kingdom	335.1	464.5	427.5	79.4	74.0	160.8	414.5	538.5	588.3
United States of America	2718.0	2810.0	2362.0	330.0	431.0	631.0	3048.0	3241.0	2993.0
DAC TOTAL	5347.0	6234.4	6984.4	1050.0	1338.6	2252.7	6408.6	7589.7	9201.1

Sources: OECD, *Development Assistance, 1972 Review* (Paris, 1972); OECD, *Development Co-operation, 1974 Review* (Paris, 1974); and data supplied by the OECD secretariat.

a. Grants and loans to developing countries in Africa, Asia, and Latin America.
b. Grants, capital subscriptions, and concessional loans by governments.
c. New Zealand became a member of DAC in 1973.

Reprinted from UNCTAD, *Review of International Trade and Development 1975* (TD/B/530/Add.1/Rev.), p. 86.

Table 6.
Financial Flows
Performance under the 1-percent target by DAC member countries,[a] 1961–1973
(Percentage of G.N.P.)

Country	1961	1963	1965	1967	1969	1971	1973	Total Flows (millions of dollars) 1973
Australia	0.54	0.49	0.59	0.87	0.69	1.33	0.52	332.2
Austria	0.06	—	0.52	0.40	0.46	0.46	0.55	152.7
Belgium	1.32	1.21	1.05	0.79	0.92	1.02	0.98	448.7
Canada	0.22	0.28	0.36	0.44	0.46	0.91	0.82	978.0
Denmark	0.35	0.02	0.14	0.28	0.80	0.73	0.58	161.3
France	2.03	1.52	1.30	1.08	1.17	0.90	1.08	2750.6
Germany, Federal Republic of	0.92	0.58	0.56	0.86	0.97	0.67	0.39	1365.9
Italy	0.47	0.57	0.39	0.33	0.94	0.74	0.34	467.0
Japan	0.57	0.34	0.49	0.61	0.72	0.92	1.38	5682.6
Netherlands	1.66	0.87	1.16	0.85	1.27	1.15	0.90	534.4
New Zealand[b]				0.21	0.32	0.33	0.30	33.4
Norway	0.23	0.24	0.38	0.33	0.42	0.49	0.48	89.5
Portugal	1.63	1.65	0.74	1.40	1.78	2.08	2.24	235.3
Sweden	0.13	0.28	0.34	0.43	0.65	0.58	0.64	319.0
Switzerland	2.09	1.30	1.07	0.81	0.50	0.89	0.62	256.6
United Kingdom	1.09	0.74	0.96	0.72	0.92	0.93	0.57	983.0
United States of America	0.77	0.70	0.74	0.65	0.45	0.58	0.54	7044.0
DAC TOTAL	0.86	0.70	0.74	0.68	0.65	0.72	0.70	21834.2

Sources: OECD, *Development Assistance* (Paris), various issues; *Development Co-operation, 1974 Review* (Paris, 1974); and information supplied by the OECD secretariat.

a. Net flow of financial resources to developing countries in Africa, Asia, and Latin America and to multilateral institutions as a percentage of G.N.P. at market prices.
b. New Zealand became a member of DAC in 1973.

Reprinted from UNCTAD, *Review of International Trade and Development 1973* (TD/B/530/Add. 1/Rev. 1), p. 85.

Table 7.

Share of major groups of countries in total world exports, 1950–1973, and projections for 1974.

Category	1950	1960	1970	1972	1973	1974[a]
			Valuation in billions of dollars			
World[b]	61.1	127.2	312.3	410.9	569.1	871.4
			Percentage distribution			
World	100.0	100.0	100.0	100.0	100.0	100.0
Developed market-economy countries	60.9	67.4	71.7	72.3	71.4	64.2
Socialist countries	8.1	11.8	10.7	10.5	10.2	9.2
Developing countries	31.0	20.7	17.1	16.4	17.5	26.0
Major petroleum exporters[c]	7.0	6.1	5.6	6.1	6.8	15.6
Major fast-growing exporters of manufactures	3.7	2.3	2.3	2.6	2.9	2.3
All other developing countries	20.3	12.3	9.2	7.7	7.8	8.2
of which:						
Large low-income countries	2.8	1.6	1.1	0.8	0.8	0.7
Least-developed countries	0.6	0.6	0.4	0.4	0.3	0.4

Sources: United Nations, *Monthly Bulletin of Statistics,* various issues, and UNCTAD secretariat estimates.

a. Assuming no change in export volume in 1974. The value of the exports of the socialist countries has been assumed to grow at the same rate as developed market-economy country exports in 1974.
b. Including unallocated amounts.
c. Prices adjusted to reflect estimated f.o.b. market prices.

Reprinted from UNCTAD, *Review of International Trade and Development 1975* (TD/B/530/Add. 1/Rev.1), p. 5.

Table 8.
Balance of payments in 1973–75 and projections for 1980 for non-oil-exporting developing countries
($ billion)

	1973	1974 (preliminary)	1975 (estimate)	1980 (projected)
Exports, f.o.b.[a]	65.3	90.1	88.3	157.3
Imports, c.i.f.	78.3	124.2	129.9	244.3
Trade Balance	−13.0	−34.1	−41.6	−87.0
Nonfactor services, net	4.0	4.8	2.7	3.5
Investment income payments, net	−6.1	−7.5	−9.7	−33.9
Private transfers	2.9	3.3	3.4	5.6
Current account balance[b]	−12.2	−33.5	−45.2	−111.8
Net capital inflow (current prices)[c]	20.3	35.9	44.0	118.6
Net capital inflow (1974 prices)[c]	——	——	——	77.9

Source: UNCTAD secretariat, based on data from the Statistical Office of the United Nations and I.M.F. and projections derived from the LINK system. For explanation of methodology, see "Trade prospects and capital needs of developing countries: report by the UNCTAD secretariat" (UNCTAD/FIN/14).

a. Assumes an annual growth rate of OECD countries of 4.8 percent for the period 1975–80 and of 6 percent for the socialist countries of Eastern Europe.
b. Excluding official transfers.
c. For the projection period these figures represent the net capital requirements and are computed as the current account balance plus an allowance for reserve increases required to maintain a constant reserves-to-import ratio.

Reprinted from UNCTAD, *International Financial Co-operation for Development* (TD/188/Suppl.1), p. 7.

Table 9.
Current-account balances[a] for major regions,
1973–75 and forecasts for 1976–77
($ billion)

Region	Actual			Forecast	
	1973	1974	1975[b]	1976	1977
OECD countries	11.4	−21.2	8.9	−3.0	5.0
Major seven[c]	(7.8)	(−10.1)	(16.6)	(2.6)	(8.5)
Other countries	(3.6)	(−11.1)	(−7.7)	(−5.7)	(−3.7)
Major oil-exporting developing countries[d]	5.6	67.0	39.0	39.0	36.0
Non-oil-exporting developing countries[e]	−12.4	−32.9	−45.2	−38.0	−38.0
Socialist countries of Eastern Europe and Asia	−2.0	−5.0	−8.0 [f]	−6.0	−5.0
Other countries[g]	−0.5	−2.6	−3.9	−4.0	−3.0
Discrepancy	2.1	5.3	−9.2	−12.0	−5.0

Sources: UNCTAD secretariat calculations, based on I.M.F., *International Financial Statistics,* February 1976; OECD, *Economic Outlook,* no. 18, December 1975; and LINK project simulations.

a. Sum of the trade balance, net services (including factor services), and net private transfers.
b. Preliminary estimates.
c. See table 1.
d. There is some uncertainty over the magnitude of the surpluses of these countries in 1974 and 1975. The Bank of England, for example, estimated them at $56.4 billion and $31.5 billion respectively. (See *Bank of England Quarterly Bulletin* 16, no. 1 [March 1976]: 23.)
e. Excluding Malta and Yugoslavia.
f. Based on data available in February 1976. Later information suggests that the deficit may be some what larger.
g. All other countries not included above.

Reprinted from UNCTAD, *World Economic Outlook* (TD/186), p. 6.

Bibliography

Books

Ali, Sheikh Rustum. *Saudi Arabia and Oil Diplomacy.* New York: Praeger Publishers, 1976.

Casadio, Gian Paolo. *The Economic Challenge of the Arabs.* London: Saxon House, 1976.

Chibwe, E. C. *Arab Dollars for Africa.* London: Croom Helm, 1976.

Demir, Solimar. *The Kuwait Fund and the Political Economy of Arab Regional Development.* New York: Praeger Publishers, 1976.

Field, Michael. *A Hundred Million Dollars A Day.* London: Sidgwick & Jackson, 1975.

Freeth, Z. *A New Look at Kuwait.* London: George Allen & Unwin, Ltd., 1972.

Fried, Edward, and Schultze, Charles, eds. *Higher Oil Prices and the World Economy.* Washington, D.C.: Brookings Institution, 1975.

Howe, James. *The U.S. and the Developing World: Agenda for Action.* New York: Praeger Publishers, 1975.

Ismael, T. Y. *The Middle East in World Politics.* Syracuse, N.Y.: Syracuse University Press, 1974.

Issawi, Charles. *Oil, the Middle East and the World.* La Salle. Ill.: The Library Press, 1972.

Jacoby, Nail. *Multinational Oil.* New York: Macmillan Publishing Co., 1974.

Kubbath, Abdul Amir. *OPEC: Past and Present.* Vienna: Petroeconomic Research Center, 1974.

Mikdashi, Zuhayr. *The Community of Oil Exporting Countries.* London: George Allen & Unwin Ltd., 1972.

Odell, Peter. *Oil and World Power.* 3rd ed., Baltimore, Md.: Pengiun Books, 1974.

Park, Yoon S. *Oil Money and the World Economy.* Boulder, Colo.: Westview Press, 1976.

Rifai, Taki. *The Pricing of Crude Oil.* New York: Praeger Publishers, 1974.

Rouhani, Fuad. *A History of OPEC.* New York: Praeger Publishers, 1971.

Sherbiny, Naiem, and Tessler, Mark, eds. *Arab Oil.* New York: Praeger Publishers, 1976.

Shlaim, Avi and Yannopoulos, eds. *The EEC and the Mediterranean Countries.* London: Cambridge University Press, 1976.

Stephens, Robert. *The Arabs' New Frontier.* London: Temple Smith, 1973.

Wall, D. *The Political Economy of Foreign Aid.* New York: Basic Books, 1973.

White, J. L. *Regional Development Banks.* New York: Praeger Publishers, 1972.

Articles

"Abu Dhabi." *The Economist,* 4 December 1976.

"Abu Dhabi." *Financial Times Survey,* 8 June 1977.

"Aid Programme." *Financial Times Survey,* 25 February 1977.

"Afro-Arab Summit." *The Middle East,* December 1977.

"Arab-African Cooperation." *The Middle East,* December 1976.

"Arab Rivalries Delay Big Sudan Project." *Saudi Gazette,* 12 February 1978.

"Arabs, Africans Agree on Close Cooperation." *Arab News,* 10–11 March 1977.

"Arabs Agree on African Aid Formula." *Arab News,* 6 March 1977.

"Arabs Set up Monetary Fund to Aid Unity." *Arab News,* 19 April 1977.

"Bank Aide Sees Reduction in Payments Imbalances." *International Herald Tribune*, 15 June 1977.

"Boom Predicted in Earnings from Saudi Cash Exports." *Events*, 23 September 1977.

"Countries in OPEC Become Net Borrowers." *International Herald Tribune*, 8 February 1978.

"Data Given on U.S. Bank Lending Abroad." *International Herald Tribune*, 8 February 1978.

"Egypt Said Asking Arabs for $1 B. in Economic Aid." *Arab News*, 8 March 1977.

"Few Protest New Oil Price Rise." *International Herald Tribune*, 29 October 1976.

"First Right Step." *Arab News*, 9 March 1977.

"Five Years of the United Arab Emirates." *International Herald Tribune*, 1 December 1976.

"Focus: United Arab Emirates," A Special Report. *International Herald Tribune*, November 1977.

"Foreign Aid Policy" (Focus on Saudi Arabia). *International Herald Tribune*, February 1978.

"Generous Foreign Aid Programme." *Financial Times Survey*, 11 February 1977.

"Gulf States Add $453 m. in Aid for Black Africa." *Saudi Gazette*, 9 March 1977.

"Hiding OPEC's Billions." *International Herald Tribune*, 18–19 June 1977.

"Investment Policy." *Financial Times Survey*, 25 February 1977.

"Kuwait—Building on Solid Base." *Financial Times Survey*, 25 February 1977.

"Merger Seems Only Hope for ASRY and Dubai." *The Middle East*, November 1977.

"Ministers Discuss Arab Monetary Fund." *Arab News*, 19 April 1977.

"OECD Warns of New Dollar Woes." *International Herald Tribune*, 14 February 1978.

"Oil." *Financial Times Survey*, 8 June 1977.

"Oil: A Looming Gap." *Newsweek*, 23 May 1977.

"Oil and the Third World." *The Middle East*, February 1977.

"OPEC Surplus." *Saudi Gazette*, 4 March 1978.

"OPEC 13 Put More of Surplus into Foreign Investments, Aid." *International Herald Tribune*, 13 May 1977.

"Petro-Dollars Surpluses." *International Herald Tribune*, 24 February 1977.

"Property." *Financial Times Survey*, 8 June 1977.

"Riyadh Reported Narrowing Gap between Income, Outlay." *International Herald Tribune*, 29 April 1977.

"Saudi Arabia: Still More Money than Power in the IMF." *The Middle East*, October 1977.

"Saudi Fund to Lend SR 130m for African Development." *Saudi Gazette*, 23 February 1977.

"Senate Staff Study Critical of Mounting Oil Debt." *International Herald Tribune*, 20 September 1977.

"$7.7 bn. Imports to Kingdom." *Saudi Gazette*, 24 February 1977.

"Spent Petrodollars." *Arabia and the Gulf*, 6 June 1977.

"Strains on World Financial System Ease." *International Herald Tribune*, 27–28 August 1977.

"The Economy." *Financial Times Survey*, 8 June 1977.

"The OPEC Supercartel in Splitsville." *Time*, 27 December 1976.

"The United Arab Emirates." *The Guardian*, 14 December 1976.

"Two Saudi Finance Aides See a Wealth of Economic Woes." *International Herald Tribune*, 30 May 1977.

"United Arab Emirates." *Financial Times Survey*, 8 June 1977.

"West Agrees to Look at Debt Aid for the Poorest." *Saudi Gazette*, 11 March 1978.

"W. Germany in Surplus in Trade with OPEC." *International Herald Tribune*, 10 February 1978.

"World Economic Forecast." *Newsweek*, 4 October 1976.

"World Economic Forecast." *Newsweek*, 26 September 1977.

Official Publications

Abu Dhabi Fund for Arab Economic Development. *Annual Report, 1976.*

Arab Bank for Economic Development in Africa. *Accord General Portant Création de la Banque Arabe pour le Dévélopment Economique en Afrique.*
———. *Annual Report 1975.*
———. *Financial Regulations.*
———. *Principles Governing the Financial Operations of the Bank.*
———. *Press Releases* (1976–78).
———. *Selected Press Clippings* (February 1976 and September 1976).
———. *Speeches by Dr. Chedly Ayari* (November 1976).
Arab Fund for Economic and Social Development. *Agreement Establishing the Arab Fund for Economic and Social Development.*
———. *Annual Report 1973.*
———. *Annual Report 1974.*
———. *Annual Report 1975.*
Islamic Development Bank. *Articles of Agreement, 1977.*
———. *The First Annual Report, 1975–1976.*
Kuwait Fund for Arab Economic Development. *Annual Report 1975/1976.*
———. *Arab Capital Markets and the Recycling of Petrofunds.*
———. *Arab Funds and International Economic Cooperation.*
———. *Basic Information.*
———. *Convention Establishing the Inter-Arab Investment Guarantee Group.*
———. *Co-operation with Consulting Firms.*
———. *Inter-Arab Equity Joint Ventures.*
———. *International Finance.*
———. *Law and Charter.*
———. *LDCs and International Bond Issues.*
———. *Some Aspects of the Oil Controversy.*
———. *The Middle East Economic Aspiration.*
———. *The Arab World—Key Indicators.*
———. *The Kuwait Fund and Trilateral Cooperation.*
———. *Towards Closer Economic Cooperation in the Middle East.*
———. *Towards Reassesment of the Recycling Problem.*
OECD. *Flows of Resources from OPEC Members to Developing Countries* (Statistical Tables), 1977.
The OPEC Special Fund. *Agreement Establishing the OPEC Special Fund.*

————. *A New Approach to International Financial Assistance.*
————. *Basic Information.*
————. *First Annual Report 1976.*
————. *Press Releases 1977.*
————. *Pricing of Oil: The Basic Facts.*
The Saudi Fund for Development. *First Annual Report.*
————. *Annual Report 1975/76*
————. *The Charter of the Saudi Fund for Development.*
The Middle East Yearbook 1977. London, England, 1976

United Nations Documents

United Nations Conference on Trade and Development. *Recent Trends in International Trade and Development* (TD/186), 5 May 1976.
————. *Current Problems of Economic Integration* (TD/B/394), 1973. (TD/B/435), 1974. (TD/B/436), 1973. (TD/B/422), 1974. (TD/B/471), 1974. (TD/B/531), 1975.
————. *Economic Co-operation among Developing Countries* (TD/B/AC.19/1), 17 December 1975.
————. *Economic Co-operation among Developing Countries* (TD/192), 22 December 1976. (TD/192/Supp.1/Add.1), 26 March 1976. (TD/192/Supp.1/Add.2), 27 May 1976. (TD/192/Supp.2), 14 January 1976.
————. *Economic Co-operation and Integration among Developing Countries* (TD/B/609), vols. 1–4, May–August 1976.
————. *Financial Co-operation among Developing Countries* (TD/B/AC.19/R.8), 29 October 1975. (TD/B/AC.19/R.8/Add.1), 29 October 1975.
————. *Joint Ventures among Developing Countries* (TD/B/Ac.19/R.5), 21 October 1975. (TD/B/AC./R.5/Add.1), 3 October 1975.
————. *Long-Term Problems of the World Economy* (Seminar Programme; Report Series no.1), November 1976.
————. *Money and Finance and Transfer of Real Resources for Development* (TD/188), 29 December 1975. (TD/188/Supp.1), 13 February 1976. (TD/188/Supp.1.Add.1), 20 February 1976.
————. *Report of the Conference on Economic Co-operation among Developing Countries (Mexico City, 12–22 September 1976)* (TD/B/628), 7 October 1976. (TD/B/628/Add.1), 8 October 1976.

――――. *Review of International Trade and Development, 1975* (TD/B/530/Add1.1/Rev.1), 1976.

――――. *Trade and Development Issues in the Context of a New International Economic Order* (UNCTAD/OSG/104/Rev.1), February 1976.

――――. *Trade Prospects and Capital Needs of Developing Countries, 1976–1980* (TD/B/G.3/134), 15 April 1976. (TD/B/C.3/134/Add.1), 31 May 1976.

United Nations Industrial Development Organization. *Comparative Study of Development Plans of Arab States* (ID/167), 1976.

――――. *Petrochemical Industries in Developing Countries* (ID/WG.34/100/Rev.1), October, 1969.

――――. *Petroleum Co-operation among Developing Countries* (ST/ESA/57), 1977.

Index

Aba al-Khail, H. E. Mohammed, 62, 156
Abu Dhabi: aid, 22, 70, 74; AFESD, 109; banks, 84; federation, 67, 69
Abu Dhabi Fund for Arab Economic Development: activities, 71–76; formation, 24, 69
Abu Dhabi Investment Authority, 69
Afganistan: aid, 73; emigrants, 68; I.D.B., 123
African Development Bank, 96, 102
African Development Fund, 53
Ahmad Mohamad Ali, 122
Algeria: ABEDA, 93; AFESD, 109, 113; aid, 40, 84; OPEC, 20; SAAPIC, 147
Al-Hamad, Abdlatif, 41, 46, 53, 111, 118
Al-Muwais, 75
Al Otaiba, Mana, 69
American Express Banking Company, 157
Arab Authority for Agriculture, 119
Arab Bank, 130
Arab Bank for Economic Development in Africa (ABEDA): activities, 91–107; aid, 25; Kuwait, 38, 40; Libya, 83; SAAFA, 143
Arab Fund for Economic and Social Development (AFESD): activities, 109–20; aid, 24; Kuwait, 38, 40, 41, 49, 50, 55; SAAPIC, 146
Arab Investment Company, 130
Arab League: ABEDA, 91, 100; AFESD, 109; Kuwait, 45, 50; OAU, 17; SAAFA 101, 143–44

Arab Monetary Fund, 40
Arab Monetary Union, 112, 119
Arab Petroleum Investment Company, 40
Arab Research Center, 99

Bahrain: Abu Dhabi, 72–73; budget, 159; Kuwait, 40
Bangladesh: aid, 27, 167; I.D.B., 123; Kuwait, 54; OPEC Special Fund, 137; Saudi Arabia, 63, 73
Bank for International Settlements (BIS): reports, 21, 162
Brazil, 63
Burundi, 74

Cairo meetings: March 1977, 17, 22; January 1974, 91
Chad: Libya, 84; Qatar, 87; SAAFA 144
Chedly Ayari, 93, 96, 103
Concessional aid, 35, 59, 67, 82
Congo: ABEDA, 98, 103; Saudi Arabia, 63, U.A.E., 67

Dubai, 70
Demir, Solimar, 117
De Vries, R. 155

Egypt: ABEDA, 93; Abu Dhabi, 72; AFESD, 109, 113, 120; aid, 25, 27, 167; I.D.B., 125; Iraq, 79; Kuwait, 36, 52; Libya, 83–84; Qatar, 86; Saudi Arabia, 59, 62; U.A.E., 67
Ecuador: OPEC, 20; OPEC Special Fund, 131–32; Saudi Arabia, 63

England: aid, 28, 161, 170
Eteki M'Boumoua, W., 99
Ethiopia, 144

Federal Reserve Board, 105
Fields, Michael, 19
Financial Times (London), 39, 68
First National City Bank, New York, 21, 153–54
Food and Agriculture Organization (F.A.O.), 15
France: aid, 28, 161
Fund for Arab Oil Importing Countries, 40

Gabon: ABEDA, 103; OPEC, 20; OPEC Special Fund, 131
GATT, 15
Germany: aid, 161, 170
Group 77, 15
Guinea: I.D.B., 123, 125

Healey Plan, 18
Holland, 170

India: Abu Dhabi, 73–74; aid, 27, 164, 167; Kuwait, 54; OPEC Special Fund, 137; Saudi Arabia, 63
Indonesia: Abu Dhabi, 73–74; I.D.B., 123; OPEC, 20; OPEC Special Fund, 131; Saudi Arabia, 62
Inter-Arab Investment Guarantee Company, 40, 50
International Bank for Reconstruction and Development (I.B.R.D.): ABEDA, 104; AFESD, 117; aid, 14, 21, 163; Kuwait, 49; Manila meeting, 12; OPEC Special Fund, 140; Saudi Arabia, 59–60
International Fund for Agricultural Development, 135
International Monetary Fund (I.M.F.): AFESD, 117; aid, 17, 155, 163; I.D.B., 123; Manila meeting, 12; oil facility, 25, 39, 59; OPEC Special

Fund, 132, 137, 140; Saudi Arabia, 60; Whiteveen Plan, 18
Iraq: ABEDA, 93; AFESD, 109; aid, 78; Kuwait, 45; OPEC, 20; OPEC Special Fund, 132; SAAFA, 144; SAAPIC, 147
Iraq Fund for Foreign Development, 79, 81
Iran: OPEC, 20–21; OPEC Special Fund, 131
Irving Trust Company, 21, 153–54
Islamic Conference, 123
Islamic Development Bank (I.D.B.): activities, 122–30; AFESD, 110, 118; aid, 25, 28; Kuwait, 38, 40; Libya, 83; Saudi Arabia, 60
Israel, 14, 60
Italy, 161

Jabal, Mahsoun B., 62
Jordan: AFESD, 113; aid, 25, 27, 167; Kuwait, 36, 52; Qatar, 86; U.A.E., 67, 72

Kuwait: ABEDA, 93–94; AFESD, 109, 118; aid, 17, 22, 24–28, 35–44, 66, 85, 159; I.D.B., 125; OPEC, 20; SAAFA, 144
Kuwait Fund for Arab Economic Development: activities, 45–56; AFESD, 116; aid, 24, 37, 41; I.D.B., 126; SAAPIC, 147
Kuwait Investment Company, 38
Kuwait Trading Company, 38

Labidi, A., 96
Lebanon: ABEDA, 94; Iraq, 79; I.D.B., 123; Libya, 84
LDC (Less Developed Countries): aid, 13, 18, 43, 161, 163
Libya: ABEDA, 93–94; AFESD, 109; aid, 78, 82–85; I.D.B., 125; OPEC, 20; SAAFA, 144; SAAPIC, 147
Libyan Arab Foreign Bank, 84

Madagascar, 98
Malaysia: I.D.B., 123–25; Kuwait, 54; Saudi Arabia, 62
Mali: I.D.B., 123; Qatar, 87; Saudi Arabia, 62; U.A.E., 74
Marshall Plan, 28, 170
M.I.T., 151–52
Mauritania: AFESD, 113; Kuwait, 53; Qatar, 86–87; SAAPIC, 147; Saudi Arabia, 60
McNamara, Robert, 96
Middle East Yearbook, 7, 27, 158, 160
Middle East Survey, 103
Mexico City Conference, 15–16
Morgan Guarantee Trust Company, 21, 153–54
Morocco: ABEDA, 93–94; AFESD, 113; Kuwait, 40, 52; Qatar, 86–87; SAAPIC, 147; U.A.E., 73
MSA (Most Seriously Affected Countries): aid, 13, 134–36, 161, 163

Nasr, Z. A., 43
Newsweek, 14
Nigeria: ABEDA, 103; OPEC, 20; OPEC Special Fund, 131
Non-concessionary aid, 20, 35, 59, 67, 82–83
Norway, 170

Oman: Abu Dhabi, 73; AFESD, 113; Qatar, 86; U.A.E., 68
Organization of Arab Petroleum Exporting Countries (OAPEC): AFESD, 113; SAAFA, 101; SAAPIC, 146–49
Organization of African Unity (O.A.U.): plan, 16; Addis Ababa meeting, 99; Cairo meeting, 92; SAAFA, 101, 143–44
Organization of Arab Unity, 91
Organization for Economic Cooperation and Development (OECD): ABEDA, 97; AFESD, 117; aid, 25, 26, 28, 29, 68, 161, 164; Develop-
ment Center, 43; OPEC Special Fund, 131, 140; reports, 21, 79, 151
Organization of Petroleum Exporting Countries (OPEC): aid,15, 18, 23, 68, 105; oil prices, 11, 152; trade surplus, 19, 20, 155, 161
Organization of Petroleum Exporting Countries—Special Fund: activities, 31–41; Kuwait, 38, 40

Pakistan: aid, 27, 167; I.D.B., 123, 125; Kuwait, 54; OPEC, 137–38; Qatar, 86; Saudi Arabia, 59, 60, 63; U.A.E., 68
Palestine Liberation Organization (P.L.O.): ABEDA, 93; U.A.E., 69
Philippines, 138
Park, Dr. Yoon, 18, 19
Petro-dollars: ABEDA, 103; Kuwait, 40, 55; surplus, 18, 20, 21, 24, 150, 154, 156, 162, 169
Program lending, 43, 47, 60, 73, 126
Project lending, 43, 47, 60, 73, 126

Qatar: ABEDA, 93; aid, 22, 26, 35, 66, 78, 85–88; budget, 159; OPEC, 20

Recycling (of petro-dollars), 18, 19, 28, 103, 162

Saeb Jaroudi, 111
Saudi Arabia: ABEDA, 93–94; AFESD, 110, 113, 118; aid, 17, 22, 23, 25, 28, 58–60, 85, 155, 159, 166
Saudi Arabian Monetary Agency (SAMA), 122–23, 128
Saudi Development Fund (S.D.F.), 61–64
Sayed Marei, 120
Senegal: I.D.B., 123; U.A.E., 73
Shah of Iran, 131
Shihata, Dr. Ibrahim F. I., 44, 132, 141
Somalia: AFESD, 113; Kuwait, 52; Libya, 84; Qatar, 86; SAAPIC, 147; U.A.E., 72

Solomon, Anthony, 157
South Korea, 63
Spain: Libya, 82–84; U.A.E., 67
Special Account for Arab Petroleum Importing Countries (SAAPIC), 146–48
Special Arab Aid Fund for Africa (SAAFA): ABEDA, 101, 106; activities, 143–45, 148
Sri Lanka, 54, 74
Sudan: AFESD, 112, 113, 119; Kuwait, 52; Qatar, 86; Saudi Arabia, 62; SAAPIC, 147; U.A.E., 73
Suez Canal, 62
Syria: ABEDA, 93; aid, 25, 27, 167; Iraq, 79; I.D.B., 123; Kuwait, 36; Qatar, 86; Saudi Arabia, 59; U.A.E., 67, 72

Taiwan, 63
Tanzania, 73, 98, 144
Technical Research Center, 126
Thailand, 138
Third World: ABEDA, 91; Kuwait, 51; OPEC, 139, 165; unity, 15
Togo, 84
Tunisia: ABEDA, 94; Kuwait, 53; Libya, 84; Qatar, 86; S.D.F., 62; U.A.E., 72–73
Turkey, 83, 123

Uganda: Libya, 84; SAAFA, 144; Saudi Arabia, 62
United Arab Emirates (U.A.E.): ABEDA, 93–94; aid, 17, 26, 28, 66–71; I.D.B., 125; Kuwait, 35; OPEC, 20; SAAPIC, 147
United Nations Conference on Trade and Development (UNCTAD): aid, 15, 25, 170; Kuwait, 44, 51; OPEC Special Fund, 140; reports, 12, 14
United Nations Development Program (UNDP): ABEDA, 97; AFESD, 114; Kuwait, 51; OPEC Special Fund, 138; U.A.E., 75
United Nations Industrial Development Organization (UNIDO): ABEDA, 97; aid, 15; Kuwait, 51; OPEC Special Fund, 140
United Nations Economic Commission for Africa (UNECA), 15
United Nations Economic Commission for Western Asia, 114
United Nations Organization (UNO): aid, 15, 16, 20, 22; Arabs, 14; Kuwait, 51; OPEC Special Fund, 137
United States: aid, 18, 28–29; Senate, 157; State Department, 151

Venezuela: OPEC, 20, 21; OPEC Special Fund, 131

Wharton Economic Forecast, 155
Whiteveen Plan, 18, 23, 155

Yeganeh, Mohammad, 133
Yemen (North): AFESD, 114; Kuwait, 53; SAAPIC, 147
Yemen (South): AFESD, 114; Kuwait, 52–53; Qatar, 86; SAAPIC, 147
Yugoslavia, 67

Zambia, 144
Zayed ibn Sultan Al Nahayan, 68